To Candy...
May you walk with wisdom,
secure upon the path He
has laid for you alone.

Jean Cowger

Paths to Dwell In

...A Devotional by...

Jean Cowger

WESTBOW
PRESS®
A DIVISION OF THOMAS NELSON
& ZONDERVAN

WestBow Press books may be ordered through booksellers or by contacting:

WestBow Press
A Division of Thomas Nelson & Zondervan
1663 Liberty Drive
Bloomington, IN 47403
www.westbowpress.com
1 (866) 928-1240

Because of the dynamic nature of the Internet, any web addresses or links contained in this book may have changed since publication and may no longer be valid. The views expressed in this work are solely those of the author and do not necessarily reflect the views of the publisher, and the publisher hereby disclaims any responsibility for them.

This book is a work of non-fiction. Unless otherwise noted, the author and the publisher make no explicit guarantees as to the accuracy of the information contained in this book and in some cases, names of people and places have been altered to protect their privacy.

Any people depicted in stock imagery provided by Getty Images are models, and such images are being used for illustrative purposes only. Certain stock imagery © Getty Images.

Unless otherwise stated, scripture quotations taken from the New American Standard Bible® (NASB), Copyright © 1960, 1962, 1963, 1968, 1971, 1972, 1973, 1975, 1977, 1995 by The Lockman Foundation. Used by permission. www.Lockman.org

Scripture marked (KJV) taken from the King James Version of the Bible.

ISBN: 978-1-9736-2350-2 (sc)
ISBN: 978-1-9736-2351-9 (hc)
ISBN: 978-1-9736-2349-6 (e)

Library of Congress Control Number: 2018903335

Print information available on the last page.

WestBow Press rev. date: 03/29/2018

A note from the author:

Born an Iowa farm girl, raised in a moral non-Christian home, I was saved at 25 and have had the privilege of walking with and growing spiritually under great and godly teachers and saints of God. I currently live with my husband of 57 years, on 5 beautiful acres filled with sculptures that represent some of his gifts and landscaped gardens that represent some of mine.

The title, "Paths to Dwell In" comes from Isaiah 58:12, the first Scripture that seemed to have been written specifically for and to me; one I've claimed for me and my family for many years now.

I have thoroughly enjoyed putting some of my thoughts and observations on paper. It will, hopefully, give you a brief look through my eyes at life and some Truths I have experienced, the conclusions or perhaps questions I have been left with. Your interpretation may be very different and that's as it should be. The Spirit is very personal to each of us, speaking what we need to know or hear. The purpose of any observation found herein comes with the hope that you might consider your own beliefs, experiences and the conclusions life has brought you thus far. I thank you for the time you will spend in my pages. May you be blessed and encouraged, perhaps challenged and ever changed into the likeness of our Lord Jesus Christ.

Complete in Him

"For in Him all the fullness of Deity dwells in bodily form and in Him you have been made complete, and He is the head over all rule and authority." (Colossians 2:9, 10)

The Lord has equipped me, filling my heart with faith, transforming my mind with His wisdom, letting me know and comprehend the secrets of Him who has redeemed me. He has restored me, established me and put all authority into my hand and care. By His power, He has spoken, and because I believe it to be so, it is mine. I take it up the authority in His Name, releasing the presence and power of the Holy Spirit into the world in which I live. In Him I am complete, having been planted with seeds of righteousness and watered with the Promises of His Word. I come behind in no good gift and shall prevail over every adversity.

Because He indwells me by the power of the Holy Spirit, He has provided and equipped me for all that I will ever need and for what life will require of me. I have the gifts, talents, wisdom, and strength to be used for His purpose; a saint who knows how to pray and encourage others, to bear up their burdens, to affirm the Truth, to understand it and walk in it by faith and with confidence. There is not one thing more that He can add to me beyond that which He has already planted with me, each seed awaiting the watering of revelation, its purpose made known to me that day and hour that life requires it. It has been set in store for a time yet to be appointed.

Oh, let me know Him as He is within this temple that is me; expressed through my heart and hands, words that speak the mystery of the Gospel of His love and a provision, His salvation, and His purpose. In Him I have found balance: humility with boldness, rest with resolve, need with provision, principles with holiness, flexibility with purpose. I know peace and am at rest for I am complete in Him who is the head of all principality and power.

There is no emptiness in me that He does not fill, no need that lies beyond His provision. His Word speaks to me, words of hope, for surely I dwell beneath the mantle of His Promise. Time has lost meaning to the one who has planted their requests in Him. Only a season lies between those moments when I let my requests be made known unto Him, and He answers. If the still voice that speaks within my heart counsels me to wait, then I shall rejoice in that season, for surely there is much more than what I ask that awaits my every step. It is this journey upon which He has set my feet. Should the answer come today, I shall rejoice; though it tarries, the giver of the Promise has not changed. I have asked and have believed in my heart that He has heard and answered; not that I have made it happen, God forbid; but that He has filled the deep desires of my heart for I have delighted myself in Him. I need not see the day of His deliverance or look upon the answer to know His Word does not return empty but is sure to bring about the things to which He sent it.

I am His beloved child and the reflection of His salvation. My life gives testimony and confesses His Promise. I shall stand and say His Name is Faithful; He who promised that the seed of the righteous would never go begging for bread. There are those I know who are still hungry for they have not reached their hand to His Bread and

His ways. But, He has not forgotten His Promise. His ear is bent low to hear me. Though the Promised season has not yet come, nor do their lips speak the words that will redeem them, the seed has still been planted and lies deep in the belly of their soul. He is faithful who promised.

I refuse to be robbed of my delight in Him; neither will I yield to the lie that drips from the accuser's lips. Why should I? He has no power that I have not given him, and I shall provide him with none. I know his power and authority were stripped and consumed by the Blood that ran down Calvary's Tree. The Blood of Jesus Christ that stayed the hand that would do evil and left him only a voice; one that hides in the darkness of sin and accuses those who wait upon the Lord God.

Because of Him, I am righteous. He calls me by name; the words there inscribed it in the Lamb's Book of Life, set down in flowing script with the same Blood that flowed from the Tree. Because Jesus Christ lives and dwells within me, the Holy Spirit stamped my name with the seal of His approval, and the Father spoke, you are my son, in whom I am well pleased. He has kept His Promise.

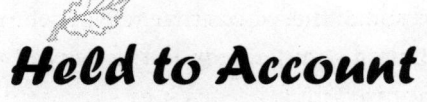

Held to Account

"The Lord is not slow about His promise, as some count slowness, but is patient toward you, not wishing any to perish but for all to come to repentance." (2 Peter 3:9)

I retired my old Bible today, well, as much as one can, I guess. Times, places, people, and memories are recorded and held within its pages. My first complete chapter begins with Genesis 4, only bits and pieces carefully taped together make up the "In the beginning..." parts and this thanks to an unthinking reader (me) and the new puppy who found it lying beside my empty coffee cup. Jeremiah says, "Thy words were found, and I ate them; and Thy words became for me a joy and the delight of my heart; for I have been called by Thy name, O Lord of hosts." (Jeremiah 15:16) Yes, she literally "ate" the Word. Now in gentle disrepair, the binding loose, the leather ragged with spots worn to holes, the pages marked with scribbled insights, underlined, highlighted – and familiar. My life, my hopes, and dreams, prayers, family, friends, and church, are written therein, planted in its pages; which both encourages me and holds me accountable to every one of them. They are the things, the ones, for whom I pray, remembering God's faithfulness to His Promise in behalf of those about whom He spoke it, and I have claimed through the years as their portion. Doing so has added life and purpose to my existence.

I wonder to whose prayer was my soul an answer? Whose knees bent and prayerfully tilled the soil of my soul, preparing it for the Seed that would soon be planted there, asking the Lord to redeem me? Family, neighbor, stranger or friend, the prayers of God's people encircle us, searching out those such as should be saved. "For the eyes of the Lord move to and fro throughout the earth, that He may strongly support those whose heart is completely His…" (2 Chronicles 16:9a) Peter says He is not willing that any should perish, but a lot had gone into the making of the day he plucked my life from destruction. Salvation is free, but not without cost.

I hope you have people in your life that hold you to a high standard of account; who love you enough to pray God's very best as your portion and will not waver in their resolve when the trials of life work His plan of Redemption within you. Some of those days will be fierce in their accusation of lack, failure, unworthiness, and doubt. It is an unearned gift that He would send another to walk beside us, to bear us up when our faith and resolve are sagging; to remind us there is more to our days than what the moment or the past accuse. Usually, those who hold us to a high account do so without a word, only the attitude of their heart, their intent, purpose, and conduct of their day to day choices speaks with an un-refutable testimony. Although saints in light, according to God's Word, they would not profess to be perfect in any way; but to my heart they are champions.

Who in your life asks the tough questions, challenges your accepted concepts, makes you dig into the reasoning behind what you believe and upon what foundation those beliefs stand? I hope you have somebody that holds you to a high standard, makes you root out and define, even defend - support, not argue - where you put your trust. These are the people you can trust with the holy things in your life, the things that have real value. These are the people who have set aside their need for your approval and acceptance;

have chanced to exchange momentary comfort for a goal of greater good. Sometimes, when our heart convicts an attitude, habit, action or word, we are tempted to avoid these brave souls who will not tickle our ears with vain platitudes. Because they believe in God's very best for us, they expect God's best from us! They are the ones who encourage excellence and authentic growth to become the standard by which we work out our salvation. Not counting growth or results, as the world measures, they affirm virtuous attitudes, godly character, integrity and purposeful accountability. Always, but especially in the beginning, they will be the ones who lovingly hold us to a higher standard and will not commend the spiritual laziness that gives license unwise liberty about lack, sin or apathy.

A life that is rewarding, rich in spiritual insight, understanding, compassion, and kindness cannot be measured by achievements - and yet it is immeasurable in its contribution to them. Grace, that unmerited favor, ministers to the needs of others according to the abundant supply that has already been tried within those "bearers of our burdens" (see Galatians 6:2) and recognized as sufficient. Grace does not need to be affirmed or rewarded to feel satisfied but has been satisfied already. How could we not encourage, first ourselves and then others, to live from such a generous position; holding each other accountable to both receive and walk in its provision?

The Final Lamb

"According to the Law, one may almost say, all things are cleansed with blood, and without shedding of blood there is no forgiveness." (Hebrews 9:22)

"Now in those days a decree went out from Caesar Augustus, that a census be taken of all the inhabited earth…and everyone was on his way to register for the census, everyone to his own city. Joseph also went up from Galilee, from the city of Nazareth, to Judea, to the city of David, which is called Bethlehem, because he was of the house and family of David, in order to register, along with Mary, who was engaged to him, and was with child." (Luke 2:1-5)

These words are vital to everyone who call themselves Christian and celebrated by many who do not. This singular event holds the same degree of meaning looking forward to spiritual history as looking back, but we rarely consider its importance in that regard. But since it is, without doubt, the single-most defining moment that ties the two together - these moments in time that separates obligation to the Law to the fulfillment of it - I find it worth taking a closer look.

Hebrews 9:22 confirms that "…without the shedding of blood there is no forgiveness." Initially, the sins of every man were answered and cleansed, his forgiveness affirmed, when Levitical priests offered a burnt offering, that of a yearling lamb without spot or blemish, as a sacrifice to God. One of the most important days of sacrifice being Passover, which commemorated a day preceding Israel's Exodus from slavery in Egypt; that day when a lamb's blood upon the doorpost assured the death angel passed over one's house (see Exodus 12:23). The need for a perfect sacrificial lamb was of highest priority to their faith; Levitical Law regarding the lamb's birth and care so strict that the need for raising them was under the care of the Temple priests at Jerusalem. These Laws were accomplished through the hands of specifically purified shepherds at a place called Migdal Eder (meaning, "Tower of the Flock") which was located a few miles outside of Jerusalem in a small village called – Bethlehem.

I know I'm taking the history of thousands of years and condensing it here, but please bear with me for I am not one to believe in coincidence or accident when examining those specifics set before us by a purposeful and intentional God. All things have message and meaning, and this one leads to the most profound Truth, that upon which the whole of Christianity rests.

Thousands of lambs were needed each year, especially on high holy days such as the Passover, so one can only imagine that flocks and shepherds were not a rare sight on the hillsides that Joseph and Mary passed on their way to fulfill the census. I wonder how many steps that donkey trod as he bore his burden southward, how many nights a small campfire gave fleeting warmth to these weary travelers; for the journey was long, the way hard and at the end of it there was no room at the inn.

For me, the image of a wooden stable that housed a nativity of various animals did not diminish when I realized it lay far from the probable truth of the stable that Joseph would have found. It was more likely, because these Bethlehem shepherds operated under Levitical law, the stable where Mary brought forth this long-awaited and promised Messiah was a clean, warm and orderly birthing cave hewn from limestone of the Bethlehem hills. The tradition of that first lamb in Egypt had been celebrated and remembered for countless years through the ministry of this small village. What more fitting place than this for the final Passover Lamb to be born, the One who would fulfill the Promise and shed His Blood in this ultimate victory over sin and death.

Although we may look to specific symbols (i.e., nativity, shepherds, angels, etc.) as a reminder of the single-most cause for our eternal hope, I find God far more intentional in His purpose of them. A golden thread connects His absolute Truth and saving Grace: from the doorpost of deliverance in Egypt, through the lambs of Migdal Eder, to the Lamb of God. These truths had been eternally woven into the fabric of salvation He bought for all who would call Him Jesus Christ, Savior.

There is much about God that we will never know so will have to take by faith. There are some things, however, that are absolutes. Those we do not assume by faith, for they are absolute: perfect, complete, pure, and real! The Scripture in Hebrews is one of those, "...without the shedding of blood there is no forgiveness." (Hebrews 9:22) The blood of lambs has passed away; the Blood of the Lamb is eternal. It calls to each of us, "That if you confess with your mouth Jesus as Lord and believe in your heart that God raised Him from the dead, you shall be saved; for with the heart a person believes, resulting in righteousness, and with the mouth, he confesses, resulting in salvation." (Romans 10:9, 10)

Saving More than a Soul

"For if while we were enemies we were reconciled to God through the death of His Son, much more, having been reconciled, we shall be saved by His life." Romans 5:10

With mild grumbling, I set about gathering what I would need to complete a job I would rather not do at all. It's not exactly the painting that I particularly dislike; it is, in this case, the preparation for it. As I looked at one glaring example of the need for immediate attention, its peeling facade undeniable, I found myself taking a trip down memory lane with regard to how I became the painter in the family in the first place. Fifty years ago, our first house and first need for a paint job found him atop the ladder and me seemingly spending more time cleaning up his drips than doing the trim that was initially my job. I finally ordered him off the ladder and finished the job. I often tease my husband that he is either a bad painter or a shrewd one, for from that day all painting chores became mine, without dispute.

Whether by design or experience, we have developed our version of submission. We certainly know and subscribe to the Scripture regarding the parts husbands and wives are to play in marriage, but somewhere along the way, the lines began to blur. As we grew, in years as well as spiritually, it became more important to submit one to the other, treating each other with respect and appreciation. We both are stronger and more complete because of the strengths, the gifts and the wisdom each brings to the whole. That my husband is my covering, I would not dispute; neither would I disparage being his helper. Who's in charge is simply not the issue. We have gratefully accepted we are better when we pull our proverbial *wagon* in tandem.

That does not mean we do not have our *moments*. Wisdom and experience do not seem a total deterrent to a word too quickly offered by a tongue whose brain was not engaged, or an ear that was not completely listening. Love, although called to be patient and kind; although it bears, believes, hopes and endures all things (see 1 Corinthians 13) must also be ready and willing to, "...cover a multitude of sins" (see 1 Peter 4:8).

Relationships will always hold overwhelming challenges; some of them seeming to thrive in the midst of trying times or adversity, while others are strained and damaged, some eventually fractured beyond repair. Marriage, which has the most significant potential for strength and growth, also carries the seed for potential destruction; making it singularly essential to be intentional about where and in what you plant your hope. A trust, once broken, stands as judge of every word and deed from that moment going forward. Only time and a miracle of God's Grace will cleanse the slate from its accusation.

Statistics bear out the proof that divorce within the church varies little from those of the *world*. Because our model for forgiveness and healing is more profound and available to every person of faith, the statistics should cause grave concern regarding them and what message they bring. Do the statistics also bear out that the many reasons for divorce are the same as those found among the lives that have not been touched by the Gospel of Jesus Christ? It's a legitimate question and concern. The plan of the devil has always been to accuse and divide us one from another; those in the church are targeted fodder for his insatiable lust. Reflection might conclude that marriage is about a whole lot more than relationship. Since the greatest strength of any society stems from those found in relationships, primarily those within our homes, has it become easier to escape than to restore? Although a healthy, vital and lasting marriage needs two people pulling in the same general direction; the platform for restoration often begins with one plus One.

We'd been married seven years when we blundered our way into a church that preached the saving Grace of Jesus Christ. Probably it could have been said that the marriage we brought with us to the church had known the best of times and the worst of times. Would we have survived as a couple apart from the personal transformation we each experienced? We have no way of saying. Would it have thrived; to that, we would confidently answer, "No"!

I've heard it said, "You can't deal water out of an empty bucket." Meaning, one cannot give to another what he/she does not have. We didn't have the wisdom or substance to fulfill our own pressing need, let alone a mate or children. Reasonably intelligent, hard-working, intentional, normal members of the human race and completely bereft of the one ingredient that gave any of it meaning or purpose. That simple prayer we each ended up praying, "Lord, forgive my sins and come into my life," saved a whole lot more than our souls!

Can You Give Me a "J"?

"Preach the word; be ready in season and out of season; reprove, rebuke, exhort with great patience and instruction. For the time will come when they will not endure sound doctrine, but wanting their ears tickled, they will accumulate for themselves teachers in accordance to their own desires." 2 Timothy 4:2, 3

I rather like most of what I see on social media, the most significant benefit being a way to keep up with the lives of those I knew in earlier days, those dear to my heart but now scattered to a variety of places for a variety of reasons. This last Mother's Day I was particularly touched by the post of a young man to his mom. In it, he expressed his appreciation for her many gifts and how blessed he considered himself to have been raised by a godly mom. I didn't know him, but I knew his mom a generation ago when she was the age of her now grown son. I remember her well; energy in abundance, bold for the Savior she'd so recently come to know, long hair, barefoot in bell-bottomed blue jeans and over-the-top in every way.

I'm so grateful for the early days of my Christian walk. Saved by the Blood of the Lamb in what began as a small neighborhood church, we barely had our spiritual feet under us when those times referred to as "the Jesus Revolution" hit and we were overtaken by young people who I will simply describe as unconventional. I have great admiration for their energy, zeal, and perseverance; but even greater appreciation for the old saints of that congregation. They were the ones who had prayed, gave, served and built this place that was now over-run with young people who knew little beyond the fact that they had had an authentic encounter with a very real Savior and it had changed them in ways that only the coming years would define. The old saints just moved over and gave them, their energy and their music a place to worship. I can only imagine that it challenged their concept of *the way things had always been*. If so, they never said.

I remember one particular Sunday evening service when the young woman I began my page with, jumped up and did the "Jesus cheer." "Give me a J..." she shouted.

Mr. Conrad just about fell off his pew; but you know, he gave her a "J."

To the young people's credit, they didn't balk at learning hymns, prayer, singing the Doxology, saying the Apostles Creed or making church attendance a regular part of their week. They grew into balanced and godly young saints, a spiritual force with which to be reckoned. I think that's why so many of them still walk with Christ today; they purposed to serve Him and His church. I never heard complaint as to whether the music *fit* their contemporary preferences or comfort, whether they felt prayer time essential or too long. They kept it about Him!

Perhaps I get a little sensitive about some of the *issues* of today's church. The music: too loud, not loud enough. The dress: too casual, not casual enough. Now it is I who is the "old saint," and I find myself wondering if my generation is giving back as good as we got. I think perhaps not, or we would hold more tightly to what is most important: that we purpose to lift up Jesus Christ, that we faithfully teach the basic principles of salvation, the life of godliness and our authority in Christ. I encourage Truth about the power of the shed Blood of Jesus, claiming God's promises, the authority He gave us over sin, the devil and his principalities and powers. Although we live in the world, let us leave social issues to the evening news. The point of the church is to teach broken people that God loves them and Christ saves them; how to receive the gift of salvation, and how to walk in it. If that's not happening through preaching, prayer, fellowship and Bible study, I have a hard time figuring the purpose of the church.

It's wearying to hear some of the *complaints* that grumble in our midst. It reminds me that there are always those among us who prefer to have their ears tickled (see 2 Timothy 4:2- 4) or "Professing themselves to be wise, they became fools." (Romans 1:22). Life is too serious, the days too evil for us to relinquish one gift, one understanding, one Truth. Let us not, O Lord, allow our spiritual liberty to make us soft on sin, to close our eyes or cover our ears.

I long for revival to sweep our hearts, our homes, and our churches; to quicken our spirit to His Spirit. May the heritage of our generation be godly homes, churches that throb with the life and energy of the newly saved, children/youth ministries that beg for more teachers and space, altars that groan under the weight of salvation prayers and repentance.

Can you give me a "J"?

Sons of Thunder

"You are from God, little children, and have overcome them; (*spirits*) because greater is He who is in you than he who is in the world." 1 John 4:4

John the Beloved did not begin his discipleship named as such; rather, he and his brother James were nicknamed "the sons of thunder," (see Mark 3:17) perhaps because of their quick temper. Scripture records that each disciple brought with them distinct personalities and gifts; failings accompanied them as well. It is left for us to interpret how their diversity both strengthened and equipped them for the job that would one day be laid in their care – to plant the church in the earth, leaving the indelible mark of salvation through Jesus Christ upon the hearts of men/women over two thousand years in the future.

Jesus was clear regarding their calling when He appointed the twelve disciples: (1) that they should be with Him (2) that He might send them forth to preach (3) and to have authority to heal sicknesses and cast out demons (see Mark 3:14-15). The calling has not changed from that day to this no matter the argument of some theologians regarding dispensations and what truths, gifts, and ministries belonged where. If Jesus said it to His disciples then, if He gave them authority, He gave it in kind to every disciple who would confess Him as Savior and Lord and believe upon His Word.

Always contemporary; time, progress and changing circumstances never diminish the truth or power of His Word.

That times have changed, I cannot argue, although it seems that those who live in this constant state of change are always searching for that which is unchangeable. Nothing stays the same for long as the rapidly swirling mixture of news, war, genocide, and terror assault our mind, heart, and soul while the cry of diverse religions seeks to divide, confuse and water down the only Truth that offers hope. Times may have changed, the battle has not. "Beloved, do not believe every spirit, but test the spirits to see whether they are from God; because many false prophets have gone out into the world." (1 John 4:1) Religion will tell you they are all the same, leading to the same God; Christ says, "For there is one God, and one mediator also between God and men, the man Christ Jesus" (1 Timothy 2:5). Religion would say that being good is good enough, while Scripture says, "For all have sinned and fall short of the glory of God." (Romans 3:23) and, "That if you shall confess with your mouth Jesus as Lord and believe in your heart...you will be saved." (Romans 10:9)

There's plenty of sin that divides the sinner from salvation, but the sneakiest thief is the one that slants the truth just enough to cause the one seeking it to miss the mark, just barely.

There is no place to hide as that which was once shocking becomes commonplace; TV, movies, videos and social media make their bid to influence, demanding large and small compromises via accepted attitudes and actions. I don't think we are called to hide, hoping to avoid the influence that comes along with living "in the world." Since strong roots are what keeps a tree from being felled by the winds of adversity, the answer must be to grow deep roots; deep enough that we become the influence by our depth of faith, honesty, character, integrity, love and personal testimony in Christ Jesus.

John did not fear the unseen or the unknown, neither did he pretend it was somehow weird to believe there was a devil, unseen spirits or "...that spirit of the antichrist of which you have heard...and even now it is already in the world" (see 1 John 4:3). He acknowledged evil but never once trembled before it, telling his spiritual generation, and the countless that would follow, their protection and power lay in the One whose Blood had saved them, redeemed them, covered and kept them. "You are from God, little children, and have overcome them because greater is He who is in you than he that is in the world." (1 John 4:4). Our only hope of enough wisdom and insight to make prudent choices and to live by them, to discern evil and avoid the pitfall of the antichrist is to know Him - to KNOW Him - and rely on the strength and wisdom of He who dwells within you by the power of the Holy Spirit.

After the Rainbow

"So he said, 'Cursed be Canaan; a servant of servants he shall be to his brothers.' He also said, 'Blessed be the Lord, the God of Shem and let Canaan be his servant. May God enlarge Japheth, and let him dwell in the tents of Shem, and let Canaan be his servant.'" (Genesis 9:25-27)

By the age of three, most that go to Sunday school have heard the story of Noah and his sons, the ark, the animals and the rainbow that represented God's promise: that He would never again destroy the world with a flood. What happened after is just as eternal, laying down the foundation that would affect people as yet unborn, battles as yet unfought and history as yet unwritten. Noah was 600 years old at the time of the flood, spent a year in the ark and then became a farmer; planted a vineyard, made some wine, got drunk and "uncovered himself inside his tent." Is that the end of one story or the beginning of another? In reality, it makes up some of each with regard to the story of Noah, making a great example of the long-lasting effects of the choices people make and the words of the decree from a father's tongue.

In more ways than one, the "rest of the story" of Noah began on the day of his birth when his father, Lamech, prophesied his son would become a farmer (see Genesis 5:29). That word was at last fulfilled after the flood. The Bible pronounces no judgment on whether Noah's choice to drink too much was wise, or not. It just states what happened and how each of his sons responded to their father's actions. Ham saw the nakedness of his father then went and told his brothers, who then backed into the tent and covered him. The Bible gives no specific interpretation of the event, just the result. That it had far reaching and long lasting ramifications indicates the sin was quite significant, which doesn't explain which sin, the father's or the son's – perhaps it was both. Noah had made a grave error when he drank too much. Having gone beyond the point of good judgment, he exposed his sin and shamed himself. Ham, instead of covering his father, perhaps judging him for it, told the tale and left the brothers to do what he should have done in the first place – cover him.

The rest of the Old Testament confirms the long-reaching ramifications of the choices made by this one father and his three sons when Noah awoke and somehow knew what Ham had done. Skipping Ham, the curse he pronounced was upon Ham's son, Canaan, who subsequently fathered the peoples that would come to be known as the Canaanites, the Assyrians, and Babylonians. They would be a thorn to Israel's existence for countless generations. The other two sons: Japheth fathered the Gentiles, and Shem's line was those through whom God's promise would find fulfillment; the Israelites (see Genesis 9:18-27).

Fast forward from Noah to the days of Joshua and Caleb; to the days where another essential chapter in God's plan unfolds, and His chosen people would finally have a land of their own. The enemies they would face were well established and well-armed, fierce and capable fighters. And just who would these descendants of Shem be facing? That would be the descendants of Ham. They had come full circle, redeeming their land from the foe that had sprung forth from a curse given in response to a hasty choice toward disobedience. God had promised a "land to dwell in," but His condition was that they were to show no mercy and drive the inhabitants from the land – completely. And here is where the breakdown presented itself again and gave place to a battle that would last throughout the victors' days. They did not obey. They compromised and gave place to the enemy to dwell within, thereby giving their enemy an opportunity to influence every part of their lives, especially their obedience to the Lord their God.

We are often tempted to think our life to be our own, our choices affecting no one but ourselves, but that's never really true. I wonder if Noah ever regretted that one night of drunkenness and the curse that subsequently altered the lives of so many. Since the words had already issued from his mouth, had already written the decree, it was too late for regret. Scripture has left that for us to ponder and perhaps wonder about the words that often issue forth from our quick lips with little thought to the lasting effect they may have.

Words do matter; whether spoken with wisdom and facts in hand, or those that rush from our lips in rebellion, anger or ignorance. How easy it sometimes seems to dance with that old part of ourselves that seeks to maintain control or comfort. It serves to make its odious claim on us because we did not "drive them out" or lay the ax to the root of some of our past choices, specific choices which subsequently claimed bits of our soul. There is no place for cohabitation between the spiritual and the soulish; for we cannot serve two masters. One must lead, causing the other to be subject to the stronger. The stronger will be the one most consistently fed. There is only one point of victory over soulish inhabitants – drive them from our land. Drive them through repentance, through His Blood, obedience, prayer, and practice – but drive them out and reclaim the land given to us by the redemptive promise of Christ Jesus.

Tiny Moments of Choice

"See, I have appointed you this day over the nations and over the kingdoms, to pluck up and to break down, to destroy and overthrow, to build and to plant." (Jeremiah 1:10)

Sitting in the sunshine just outside the back door, a cup of coffee in hand and my camera close by, I wait in the hope of catching a shot of this tiny Hummingbird that always lands on the same branch before making her way to the feeder. It is a fresh and glorious morning that meets my husband as he opens the back screen door, steps onto the porch, stretches out his arms and says, "Morning, Lord. What do You have in mind for us today?" If you were to say that to yourself right now, what would be your instant internal response? Would your heart leap with eager anticipation with the promise of the day? Or, does weight and dread course its dark tendrils across your chest and squeeze a bit of life from your soul? Does hope spring eternal in your soul for all each day will hold?

You've probably heard the adage about some seeing the glass as half full, some half empty; supposedly showing if we have a negative or positive outlook. I maintain it is likely more important to determine what's in the glass.

I'll come back to it, but I'm going to leave the glass half full at the moment and take us to 2 Samuel 18 for a look at David's life and

Absalom, his son. For all the hand of God had brought to his life through his days leading up to becoming king, David did not handle being a king as well as he'd managed the process of becoming a king; his "after" included adultery and murder, the seeds of his sin following him into the lives of his children. That's often the hardest part of the destructive seeds we sow in life, watching the fruit of them sprout in the lives of our next generations. Incest marred the palace, and then revenge as the younger son, Absalom, avenged his sister by having the guilty elder son murdered; thereby also setting himself in line for the throne. I maintain again that it mattered not so much that the glass was half full or half empty, it mattered what was in the glass. This glass was half full of intrigue, betrayal, power struggles, lies and the war that followed them. This particular scene ended with Absalom dead, killed by one he thought to be his ally. Finding Absalom dead, two messengers speed off to take the news to the king; one messenger appointed, one self-appointed. It happened that the self-appointed messenger arrived before King David first. When asked what he saw, he replied "...I saw a great tumult..." (2 Samuel 18:29b) He understood none of what was in this particular *glass*; what had brought them to this point, what it meant or the impact it would have. His view was so incomplete and his subsequent report so skewed that he omitted the whole purpose of his mission – Absalom was dead. Some are just not to be trusted with reporting the truth, not because they are not trustworthy, more likely because they have no clear understanding of what the whole of the reality is, or precisely what it means. They miss the point.

It is crucial that we pay attention to what we make room for in our day to day, sometimes moment by moment. Do we miss a significant portion of our life because we skipped too quickly past those tiny moments of choice that quickly come and pass in kind? Have we lost the joy of the present because we saw only the "tumult?" I'm not sure precisely what David expected to harvest from the family legacy he established, but I'm fairly sure it wasn't the portion that was his reality. The choices he made by the counsel of his flesh limited the whole of what he might have reasonably expected to harvest for David would not build the Temple to the Lord God that had been his dream. Thankfully, God did not leave him where some of his choices had taken him.

It is not unusual that any given day will hold disappointments and challenges, no matter what attitude with which we met the day. Life always has a measure of the unpredictable and the uncontrollable. Most of these will be very minor, mostly just frustrations or small inconveniences. It is, however, those first moments of any battle that will form our perception of the whole. We would be well advised to look for the point of revelation in it and not to the "tumult" that will always attend it. I doubt that one is born either optimist or pessimist. Our outlook on life is a learned behavior, honed bit by bit by what experience has exposed us to and how we learned to cope with it. Although true that many who learned to answer it with dread or fear did so with good reason, the circumstances that form many of our responses were real enough. But, to allow the memories or experiences planted in our life - whether by our hand or that of another - to become a constant counselor to our responses is to relegate oneself to a life of bondage. The Blood of Jesus Christ paid for every one of them that you confess and lay in His nail-pierced hand. You need not remain a debtor to the past. Redemption brought David's hard-won truths a lineage that included Jesus Christ. By His Blood, we too are in His line.

The Toothless Lion

"Be of sober spirit, be on the alert. Your adversary, the devil, prowls about like a roaring lion seeking someone to devour." (1 Peter 5:8)

Most of us have what might be a secret admiration for Peter. Perhaps not the denial part, we don't want to go that far, but he's just so real, so human, and with that, we do identify. No matter how much we love the Lord; there are times when our flesh runs ahead of our love for Him. That was pretty much why Peter denied Christ. He had such high hopes that the Messiah would change the earthly kingdom as well as the heavenly and it only led to the Crucifixion; it seemed so final. Unable to understand beyond the moment, overwhelmed with the pain, loss, and disappointment, he denied and ran.

It was this experience more than any other that changed Peter. Although he'd spent many days at the side of Jesus, had heard and was nourished by His Words first hand, Peter failed in the face of this great trial for it touched depths that had not yet been tried by fire. All of the disciples reacted in different ways to Christ's ultimate sacrifice. If we'd look, we'd probably identify with one of them. We hope if faced with a similar reality that we'd do better, but none of us know how deep Grace goes in us until faced with a life-changing challenge. We live hoping we'll be brave and righteous; but, when pain and disappointment argue themselves to be the only dividends of our life-investment, it's not so easy to rejoice and see beyond those moments. If we are honest, most of us find it easier to live in the shallow end of the pool hoping, as the disciples did, that somehow Jesus is going to alter the circumstances of our earthly lives. It is not circumstances He came to change, but us in the midst of them. Walking with Him soon teaches us how little we know about the more profound things of Christ - long before we find out what *more profound* really means.

When we come together on a Sunday morning all clean and shiny, we have no idea what each has brought with them beneath the smile and cheerful, "I'm fine, how are you?" That each one that came together to worship has brought some burden with them, we can most likely be assured. If not our health, finances, broken heart or cares, our heart is first caught and then engaged by the pain, needs or woes of others for whom we care. Somehow suffering feels like a bad thing, something to be avoided or dismissed as soon as possible. It's hard for our human consciousness to accept that it could, in any way, be good for us; that in its fires we are tried and refined, purified and focused. As much as our flesh may whine or seek to dismiss the Truth, it can neither be rejected nor denied.

Grief and failure refined Peter, strengthened his understanding and his resolve. The weight of what had happened, the arrest, beating, and Crucifixion of Jesus and the authority that was now Peter's, fell with unerring precision on the seed that had been planted and nurtured through the many days of intimate fellowship with His Lord. That's what ultimately came to his aid when faced with uncertainty; those things that had been planted in Him long before he needed them. He finally *got it*. That's why he speaks with such authority about sharing in the sufferings of Christ beginning with the words of Peter (see 1 Peter 4:12), telling us we shouldn't be surprised at the "fiery ordeal" of life.

In the Book of Luke, Jesus had made a curious comment to Peter. "Simon, Simon, behold, Satan has demanded permission to sift you like wheat; but I have prayed for you, that your faith may not fail; and you, **when once you have turned again**, strengthen your brothers." (Luke 22:31, 32) Jesus was neither surprised nor concerned at Peter's denial because He knew, "... that all things work together for good to them that love God. to them, who are called according to His purpose." (Romans 8:28) Even though it's hard not to get caught up in the moment when we face life's challenge, we should not deny or seek to throw away our greatest struggles or darkest moments, thinking them failures of no value. The man who penned the words "suffering" and "humility" of 1 Peter was no longer the same man who had made so many brash and untried promises – three denials stood between those two moments in time. Peter writes as one closely acquainted with the sometimes rocky process of redemption. Reading this, one cannot help but notice that this is not the same strong-willed, brash and impetuous fisherman that followed Jesus away from the Galilean shore, nor was he the same self-confident man that said, "You are the Lord" when Jesus asked, "Who do you say that I am?" (See Luke 9:20). Two life-altering encounters had acquainted Peter with failure, grief, and transformation: the suffering and denial that surrounded the Crucifixion, and the revelation that came when the Holy Spirit revealed all things, filling him in the Upper Room.

Peter wrote, "Be sober in spirit, be on alert. Your adversary, the devil, prowls about like a roaring lion, seeking someone to devour." (1 Peter 5:9) He wrote from the first-hand experience of personal suffering, repentance and a final and victorious restoration of authority. From that position, he counseled, "But resist him, firm in your faith...and after you have suffered for a little while the God of all grace, who called you to His eternal glory in Christ, will Himself perfect, confirm, strengthen and establish you" (see 1 Peter 5:8-10). Amen!

Stretched Beyond Imagination

"When he entered the house, the blind men came up to him, and Jesus said to them, 'Do you believe that I am able to do this?' They said to Him, 'Yes, Lord.' Then he touched their eyes, saying, 'It shall be done to you according to your faith.'" (Matthew 9:28, 29)

It is in chapter 9 that Matthew recounts, "...He saw a man, called Matthew, sitting in the tax office; and He said to him, 'Follow Me!' And he got up and followed Him." (Matthew 9:9) No details were given as to what Matthew might have been thinking in those moments. I wonder how many miracles he had already seen, miracles that must have stirred his soul and spoke testimony of this man of whom it was said; He is Lord. How many words had Matthew heard Jesus speak, words his heart confirmed as Truth that must be acknowledged? We are left to imagine that Matthew, in his tax gathering duties, had seen and heard much regarding this man from Galilee; enough that when Jesus called him, Matthew's faith rose to the challenge he dropped everything and followed Him.

I think Matthew, a fascinating choice for a disciple, but then I guess all of us are when you consider our individual and diverse characteristics. Matthew was not one of the *beautiful people*. He was despised by his community because of his job and his association with Rome, making relationships suspect and near impossible, one would suppose. Tax collectors either kept to themselves or socialized with other tax collectors. He now found himself part of a tight-knit group of apostles. It is entirely possible his new-found faith stretched him in ways he could not have imagined. Perhaps that's why he is so purposeful and intentional as he records and recounts the ministry and miracles of Jesus; his whole life had prepared him for that singular moment when he stepped across the line of the human convention into the unknown of faith. Faith cost him everything: pride, old habits of the flesh, his career and the practical sense of authority and power that had come with his job. As a tax collector, he could not have been the kind of man who felt compassion for the condition of the humanity he walked among every day; but he had been an observer of them, perhaps judged their lives and assumed circumstances. He knew the woman that touched the hem of Jesus's garment had suffered her illness for twelve years; saw the tentative touch upon Him, perhaps understanding her need and her faith because he had so recently stood on the other side of it.

There's nothing very realistic about faith; it requires one to forgo both senses and experience in exchange for the unseen and the unknown. One can view the hope that comes through faith to be akin to the parable of the talents in Matthew 25:15-28; everyone has a measure, a seed of faith given by God (see Romans 12:3) but increasing that portion depends on how we use it and where we put it. Everyone walks by some degree of faith; either engaging their ability and resources to meet the needs or, acknowledging their limitations, are wise enough to release the need to another Source. Since our resources often pale in the light of most needs, why would we hold so tightly to control?

For the Pharisees, the religious of the day, the pompous control and respect for their position was all they had. They studied, knew and legalistically held with an unbending bias to long-established rules, to their status in society and their very lifestyle of Law. They judged that their beliefs were being spurned and challenged by this upstart Jesus and his band of rag-tag nobodies who went about the country healing, raising from the dead, casting out demons and forgiving sins. This Teacher was even using Scripture to challenge their tightly held beliefs, saying, "I desire compassion and not sacrifice," (see Hosea 6:6) for I did not come to call the righteous, but sinners." (Matthew 9:13) That those of us sinners, saved by Grace, have the same potential to sit just as smugly upon our salvation in buildings made by hands has always been the challenge for the flesh-nature of those of us who make up the church. Apathetic satisfaction quickly forgets, "It is not those who are healthy who need a physician but those who are ill." (Matthew 9:12) Perhaps we err most often in our walk of faith by holding it too tightly when it calls to be set free.

Matthew watched and recorded those who suffered but were made whole, were possessed and delivered, lost and then found. May their cries be heard and met by those *Matthews* of our day, always. Let us never forget and faithfully proclaim the saving Grace that points the way to the Savior.

The Narrow Gate

"Enter through the narrow gate; for the gate is wide and the way is broad that leads to destruction and there are many who enter through it. For the gate is small and the way is narrow that leads to life, and there are few who find it." (Matthew 7:13, 14)

I sat this morning to write my thoughts concerning this verse and before I had even finished writing the reference, I got *the call* and was challenged to put these words into action before I'd even had time to ponder their meaning. Life is like that. It's a beautiful day, kids out the door, dog fed, a few moments to yourself with the Word, your thoughts and your pencil. Then, you get *the call* that demands something of you, someone with a need stops by, the mail brings bad news and an otherwise tranquil day turns needy and turbulent, trying to suck your peace and emotions into the fray. Life is a never-ending opportunity to make choices; some will be eternal.

I believe Jesus Christ is not only the door to eternal life; He is the gate to a redeemed life, one that is reclaimed and completed, in the right here and now. He is the narrow path, yet He does not constrain - although He does define - offers not fewer choices but choices more purposeful, the results less ambiguous.

One never stays on the narrow path because he has no other choice; he's already had too much to choose from, has made too many decisions that either left him in the cross-hairs of destruction or the never-ending maze of regret. No, he who walks the narrow road does so by purposeful intention; has set his eye on a surety beyond what life had held thus far.

Perhaps that is the uncomplicated part; the realization that life doesn't hold much more than a vague glimmer of what had made up our youthful dreams. We generously laid our future in those hopes and dreams. Although some may have dreamt of fame and fortune, most were more reasonable: a good job, family, a vacation or two and happiness. Everyone was happy in their dreams, whether famous or a regular Joe, all were happy! Maybe that is the stuff dreams are made of, that thirst to be happy and satisfied with whatever path life had taken.

It isn't long before *unhappiness* begins to dog our steps. That's when the first great temptation will present itself for our consideration. When *happiness* seems to run one step ahead of us, most often the urge is to catch up and to try a few new things that might help it along. A little drink or smoke, a pill, fling, or shopping spree, a small change that doesn't seem like such a bad thing and for a brief moment "Happy" is quiet – but probably not for long. "Happy" is never fed from the outside.

When those moments of self-realization first begin to present themselves, the ones that argue that life isn't cooperating with our storybook plan, it is not unusual that the drives of our flesh-nature are labeled the culprit, but sometimes I'm not so sure. If one were to look a little deeper, one might conclude that the soul - the seat of our emotions - was the real culprit and the flesh is merely his/her servant. What we call *unhappiness* springs out of our emotions. When fear, doubt, envy, dis-satisfaction – you know, emotions – begin to speak to us, our flesh quickly goes into action to try to fix it, to quiet the incessant nagging. Soon that helpful flesh has conveniently established a pattern or habit of *fix* and, since it hasn't fixed anything, it tries a little harder to take one more drink or pill, go here, run there, buy this, try that. These are a fair example of a "wide gate" - the flesh seeking to satisfy the soul.

The narrow gate works the other way around. Jesus goes straight to the problem. He saves the soul, and the flesh becomes His servant – if we are wise enough to allow it. The narrow gate that leads to life is always the same: stable, secure, never-changing, based on a hope beyond ever-changing flesh or emotions. We, human children, look so diverse; but our fundamental nature is all the same. No matter the symptoms, the final diagnosis is that we are lost and cannot save ourselves. The narrow gate is the answer, but the mystery of it is this: where the wide gate is easy enough to find and enter, once through it narrows to a choking prison; whereas the narrow gate, being harder to find, opens to a broad path of liberty.

Having traveled both paths – narrow is the preferred journey for one who likes freedom. How's that for an enigma?

Agreement by Consent or Silence

"A man has joy in an apt answer, and how delightful is a timely word!" (Proverbs 15:23)

Some things come to our lives for a lifetime; some things only for a season. It's important to know the difference.

No matter our position in life, rich or poor, ethnicity or attitude; all who hold to life and living will have seasons of diversity and change will be a constant companion. No one escapes the challenges of life, good times and bad. We never know, even when the face or voice that meets us is cheerful, what another holds in the depths of their heart; what burden they may carry or loss with which they may be trying to come to grips. Emotions are often volatile in this high tech, diverse and complicated world. Opinions, beliefs, traditions and a variety of prejudices give rise to discontent, unrest, anger, and war.

As Christians, those who believe and have accepted salvation by the shed Blood of Jesus Christ, we should be drawn into a fold of oneness and solidarity with other believers. Because of doctrines, judgments and distrust, isolationism is more often the case; minds and hearts closed. It damages our testimony to a fallen world and efficiently diminishes a combined front of strength to a world that grows bolder in their opinions and evil strategies week by week. We are beginning to hear of those who must live their faith-lives in fear and hiding. Torture and martyrdom are words that have leaped out of the pages of history to take their place in today's news. These kinds of realities are sobering and should be sufficient cause to set aside diversities that make no eternal difference and perhaps consider those things we have in common to be more critical.

Most of us will never be a position of power in the physical sense, to render a change in the politics and policies that run the governments of our nations; even less the factions that bring both verbal threats and violent confrontations to peace and safety throughout the far reaches of our world.

We have no power to render change – out there or over there! We have, however, been given a great deal of dominion to affect change: in our own heart and attitudes and within the circle of lives we touch at work, school, neighborhoods, and shops. That we agree is not required; but acceptance of and tolerance for differences, cultures, even beliefs, is vitally important. Accepting one another becomes the platform from which people begin to understand one another – any hope of influence starts there. We may be shocked, infuriated, aghast or confused at acts of violence, but no one became a riot of intolerance alone. Somewhere along the line of every individual that has given himself/herself to hatred, bigotry or obsession was the seed of a falsehood that was encouraged to fester and grow because it was agreed to: by consent or silence.

We are not powerless. A place to start:

Prayer! God is not surprised at our world or our need. An agreement is a powerful tool to effect change, but it requires a willingness to set aside our opinions and pre-conceived notions for a higher purpose. Our ideals and our views do not provide an answer, but they certainly do limit the possibilities of finding one. Most hold to prejudice out of fear, which binds us more tightly to the thing we fear than to the probability there is more to our lives on which we could agree. No matter how small the seeds of the agreement, they provide a plateau from which God may work and then move. He did not *need* our help when long ago He established that man would be interactive - have dominion - in the affairs of earth. The Cain and Abel side of life was never God's plan, but then, man is often left asking His help to restore what came after choices that had been ill-advisedly made. His plan has not changed, so let us pray.

Thoughtful consideration! Since our interaction is limited to individuals, we have considerable power to make life - theirs and ours - a little less burdensome by graciously accepting our differences and being genuine in our choice to do so. It shouldn't be easier to respond to various cultures and beliefs with indignation, fear, and intolerance. How might that influence the world for Christ? Did He not eat with publicans and sinners? Influence does not require that we understand or believe the same, but often the gentle gift of kindness and tolerance does leave enough space to allow God to begin to sort things out.

That we're a frustrated people is an understatement! And yet, "... how timely is a delightful word." That's about the only control we have, the only response we can offer to a world near void of consideration, intentional tolerance, and kindness. It may not change much, but it will change some. We do not control the potential that lies within those seeds we plant. We are just called to cast them abroad into our world. For, "In Him, you have been made complete, and He is the head over all rule and authority." That's an excellent place to start!

Crinkled at the Corners

"I am the Lord, I have called you in righteousness, I will hold you by the hand and watch over you, and I will appoint you as a covenant to the people, as a light to the nations." (Isaiah 42:6)

I often wonder at the working of the Lord and am convinced His Plan for us was laid with precision and care before we knew to seek Him. When I first met the man who would one day be my husband, I'm not exactly sure what it was about him that changed the way I saw both him and me. Let's just say he caught my attention. Let's just say it was his well-formed and capable-looking hands and his warm brown eyes that crinkled at the corners that stayed with me past our first meeting. To say we are opposites would be accurate but to say we are entirely compatible would be correct as well.

Neither of us knew Christ as Savior back then, but that He orchestrated our beginnings, I have no doubt. We were in our seventh year of marriage when we opened our hearts and lives to Christ. I cannot begin to number or explain the changes in us, our home, our path, our choices; but they were profound and life-changing.

As part of a growing church – one that had exploded with revival within our community – meant many in our congregation were close in spiritual years. That did not always translate into spiritual maturity. All of us were in the process of learning who we were, what gifts and talents lay awaiting discovery just beneath the carefully constructed façade each had brought with him to this new life of which we knew little. Slowly, old habits began to crumble as we grew and changed. We started to comprehend what the Bible means when it speaks of laying aside "...the old self with its evil practices." (Colossians 3:9b) The *self* we brought to Him slowly disappeared as we learned more about this new life of Jesus Christ that dwelled within us by the power of the Holy Spirit.

I admired one who could stand and preach – my husband did not. Another could quote long passages of Scriptures; another prayed with eloquence and power – my husband did not. You see where I'm going with this – I was comparing gifts and it was my guy who seemed to come up short.

We lived close to the church so always walked. One day as we made our way across the church parking lot toward home I felt a bit as Paul must have felt as the scales fell from his eyes and he saw the light. As we walked and chatted, my husband stopped to pick up a discarded bulletin and a used foam cup, his actions continuing until he had a handful. These words rose inside of me, "On this Lord's day, many walked by the litter in My parking lot and did not see or stop to pick it up." And then the words, "He that is faithful in the least of these things ... I will make him ruler over many things" (see Matthew 25:21).

I began to see my husband in a whole new light that day. No one would ever see the trash he picked up, or publicly proclaim his contribution; neither would they call it a ministry or a gift. He didn't need that. He was faithful in little things because it was enough for him to cheerfully do whatever came his way, those small things that are necessary, but most often overlooked. As the years have gone by, my appreciation has only grown for his many gifts and talents; but more so for his attitude and service. I've heard many testimonies from people who came new and uncertain to visit our church and found the courage to return because of a handshake from some well-formed, capable hands and a sincere welcome from a pair of warm brown eyes that crinkled at the corners.

He is a man who hears the beat of another drum, entirely comfortable in both his personal and spiritual skin. I remember a time when he'd been asked to pray. He did so, said "Amen" only to have someone remark they hadn't heard him. If he was self-conscious or undone by the comment, I couldn't say; his only response was that he hadn't been speaking to them. His easy wit and sharp sense of humor go a long way toward his ability to speak Truth without giving offense.

We err if we allow ourselves to despise the day of small things (see Zechariah 4:10). As God does not consider one sin to be more grave than another; neither does he count each gift to have more or less value than another. He does, however, consider the condition of our heart when we lay our gifts before Him. He wants, His world needs, every gift to be in action for it is this body ministry of gifts generously given that clears the way for sinners to walk the path to where He is and cares for them after they get there. Is not the hope of each of us to one day stand before the Lord and hear the words, "Well done thou good and faithful servant…"

The Other Way Around

"...we have not ceased to pray for you and to ask that you may be filled with the knowledge of His will in all spiritual wisdom and understanding." (Colossians 1:9b)

It seems that eventually, as the years add up and the experiences - the good and the bad - stack up, most humans eventually get around to pondering some pretty deep questions, "Why am I here?" "What is the purpose of my life?" "Should I?" "Could I...?"

I guess my own experience was predictable in many ways. I did not grow up unscathed by circumstances or my reactions to them. Most of us could say the same, in varying degrees. Life touches us, challenges our ability, inner fortitude, know-how, mental and physical strength and endurance. And, without exception, those things we know and have lived will eventually leave us wanting. Invariably, we come up damaged in some area because there was not enough of us to fill what was required to do, to be, or from which to recover. Had I been asked why I was here, I could not have answered. If asked what I wanted out of life, my answers would have reflected your own, most likely. No matter the choice of words, most boil down to wanting pretty much the same: to be happy, secure, provided for - or able to provide - to have a purpose, to be safe. My goal became "Nirvana" which was supposed to be simple and attainable. I became a poster child for what the middle class considered American success – an ideal on the outside, a hollow mess in the inner. Few could adequately describe what the gaping hole on the inside feels like, the one which success, things or people cannot fill. We desire to maintain control in a world where control does not exist. We have no words to adequately describe emptiness, so we merely say we are not happy.

Finding Christ as Savior finally answered that need I had but could not have put into words. I now belonged to something beyond my meager internal resources and the sense of being completed in Him brought life where chaos had so often threatened destruction. Salvation also brought a whole new depth and meaning to the questions I'd long suffered about life and purpose; the difference being I now had a resource for answers and help to find them.

I think humans very often get life backward; adding church and spiritual things with the hope of rounding out our physical being when it is decidedly meant to be the other way around. Because the breath of God gives life to what would be a pile of dust without it, we are all spiritual beings foremost; our physical body and our life-experience only a springboard to eternity in heaven or hell. Choose wisely!

One could well imagine the Apostle Paul wrestling with the same questions as we, pondering purpose and place as he lays out seven paths to spiritual wisdom and understanding in the words written in Colossians 1:9-12:

- Live in a manner that will honor the Lord.
- Please Him in all things.
- Let your life bear good fruit.
- Increase in the knowledge of God.
- Be strengthened with His power.

- Attain steadfastness and patience, with joy.
- Give thanks, for you share in His inheritance.

Without a doubt, living according to this plan would not only qualify the character of one's life but give it a purpose that reaches beyond self. It is impossible to attain – if left to our understanding and capabilities. Were it not for the Blood of Jesus Christ that cleanses us from sin and the Holy Spirit who dwells within this temple of flesh; it would be impossible to please Him. But, He has chosen, "...to give you complete knowledge of His will and to give you spiritual wisdom and understanding." We usually tend to make this way more difficult than it needs to be. We don't have to *find* His will or *seek* His wisdom. They consist more of allowing Grace to happen in and to us than making it happen because of what we think or do.

Christ wants to express Himself in and through us. He uses the joys, sorrows, and challenges of our life as occasions to express Himself in and to the little circle that is our humanity. It is imperative to any design that the intended goal is understood before its purpose becomes clear. Who better to reveal the form, function, and intent of God's perfect plan than He who knew us before we were formed in our mother's womb (see Jeremiah 1:5)?

Find Out if He Means It

"And my God will supply all your needs according to His riches in glory in Christ Jesus." (Philippians 4:19)

My husband and I had been married nearly seven years when life brought us to that point where we first faced the reality of our own choices and uncertain mortality. Soon after, we both knelt at the altar of the old Falls Avenue church and prayed the sinner's prayer; confessing our sin, asking forgiveness and invited Jesus into our heart and life. It was a simple prayer, to be sure, for we were simple people and could not argue that we were in need of a Savior.

I'm not sure the Lord ever saved anyone who knew less about spiritual things than either one of us because we knew nothing beyond knowing that He was no longer *out there* but now lived *in here*, as we patted our heart. We had found a place where we fit among the young families, as ignorant about God as we, and old saints who smiled at our ignorance and slid over to let us in – and in we did slide. We jumped in with both feet, eager for places we could be a part, soaking up singing and sermons, hamburgers after Sunday night service and fellowship with others as hungry as we.

I remember asking my husband one evening as we walked home from church, "Do you think we're going to get real *religious*"? He answered, "We are going to do this all the way, or we're not going to do this at all."

Unlearned man in the way of spiritual knowledge, perhaps, but he was not unwise. Nothing ever really works when given half a heart, half a chance. And, we never did become *really religious* but began a process of change and transformation that is still a constant companion these many years later.

Perhaps one of our most life-changing seasons happened rather early in our faith-journey when my husband was laid off from his job during an "economic downturn."

My reaction: "What are we going to do?"

His response: "God says He will supply all our needs. We're going to find out if He means it."

We were still new Christians, knew little about faith or spiritual Truths, really, and this was the first time our faith had met much of a challenge. Our income became significantly reduced, and in the coming two years we eventually used up unemployment benefits and had no other resource – but God.

Now, my husband has always been *artsy*, and without a day-to-day job to go to, he had a lot of extra time on his hands. One day during that time he set up an old wood lathe which he powered with a motor from a junked washing machine. Not fancy but he began turning out beautiful candlesticks, which I finished in the garage. We would set up a table at whatever art show or flea market we could find on the weekend - and the candlesticks sold, and our house payment was always paid without fail each month, our needs more than met.

Early on we found out that the Word of God is not only real but precise. He means what He says - if we can believe it. Beyond these life-changing revelations concerning God and His Word, we found out a lot about ourselves in this process. This particular journey lasted a little over two years. We found out about fear and doubt; we also found out about faith and perseverance – and a whole lot regarding gifts that had lain hidden in us until circumstances forced the opportunity for them to be made known to us.

I do not mean to diminish the challenges that accompanied those days. Walking in new-found Truth is rarely the same as a walk in the park. It cost us something to believe! But, it soon became apparent as we continued to persevere that we were adding more to our spiritual, emotional and physical storehouse than any cost we might have incurred. Those days changed us forever. We've often wondered if we ever would have found those parts of us had we not known those days of lack and challenge. The result of those experiences opened a path to a whole new world, one that has expanded and fulfilled us in ways we could not have imagined before or in the midst of them. We went on to open and run a diverse and well-appointed art shop, traveled extensively, met lots of unusual and interesting people, my husband went to college and ended his career as a very prolific and accomplished sculptor.

Out of one season of adversity and a seed of faith, we found out God meant what He said, and we had become privy to His faithful provision. We were also enriched, encouraged and expanded in the process, far beyond what we could have imagined or thought to ask.

It Ended On a Tree

"For there is one God, and one mediator also between God and men, the man Christ Jesus, who gave Himself as a ransom for all, the testimony given at the proper time." (1 Timothy 2:5, 6)

God's plan has always been intentional and purposeful, never changing; one generation upon the next faithfully planting into the foundation of Truth and prophecy that Christ would one day fulfill and complete on the Cross. I often relate our spiritual history to a finely woven tapestry; each thread being laid down with thought and care until the final picture, the one held in the mind of the weaver from the beginning, emerges from what had seemed unrelated threads. Only then do we finally see and know the whole of it.

In the beginning, God created and out of chaos came order. Divine Order held every ingredient man would ever need to fulfill God's plan for all of creation. Into his care, He had given everything and, although mankind had it all, *all* was contingent on this one Word of restraint. "The Lord God commanded the man, saying, 'From any tree of the garden you may eat freely; but from the tree of the knowledge of good and evil you shall not eat, for in the day that you eat from it you will surely die.'" (Genesis 2:16, 17) But woman and man did eat of the tree and into the midst of order came – chaos.

It was not the tree itself that was evil; God's nature cannot create evil. The tree was but a symbol that reflected the weight of responsibility carried within the free will He had gifted into the soul of every man/woman; the gift to choose what or whom we will serve. With every provision at his fingertips, would a mankind decide to accept less? Evidently, they will, for they ate of the tree.

God, intentional and purposeful, never leaves loose ends hanging. Biblical history confirms that even though mankind fell from Grace and God had to punish their disobedience, He provided a way that every loss might know atonement, and every penalty might be redeemed, even the smallest. It's a good reminder that although man's separation from God began with a tree - of the knowledge of good and evil – the hope of redemption was carried through the years by the Acacia tree that lent its wood to the Ark of the Covenant which carried God's promise and ended with resounding finality upon a Tree - the Cross.

Scripture is full of symbolic truths, so by them, men might always be reminded. The Ark of the Covenant was a type or representation of the Messiah, in whom atonement and redemption would eternally rest. Its presence among the people both confirmed and reminded them: God's Covenant Promise with His chosen people, His presence dwelt among them, He was a God of mercy. In it rested: (1) The 10 Commandments - for life and godliness (2) Aaron's rod – a representation of authority (3) Manna - provision for the body (4) The book of the Law of Moses – provision for the soul.

As we seek to understand it we must then realize God's Word doesn't leave vital truths flapping around untied to His greater or completed purpose. Always intentional, ever purposeful, He weaves every strand into the victory of redemption that Jesus Christ purchased with His Blood on the Tree that was Calvary. Consider these words from Genesis, "...Cursed is the ground because of you;

in toil you will eat of it all the days of your life. Both thorns and thistles it shall grow for you…" (Genesis 3:17, 18) Because of Adam's disobedience the ground was cursed and would produce thorns and thistles. I'm therefore prone to consider that even the Crown of Thorns that men laughingly put upon the head of Jesus served a redemptive purpose, satisfying even this smallest of curses. That is the nature of Jesus Christ – redemption.

Often it is history that testifies to the long-lasting foolhardy and hastily made choices of Mankind. Consider the death of Abel at the hand of his brother, Cain. "What have you done? The voice of your brother's blood is crying to Me from the ground. Now you are cursed from the ground, which has opened its mouth to receive your brother's blood from your hand." (Genesis 4:10, 11) The Blood of Jesus Christ spoke Redemption to ALL that the Fall had touched. When Christ's Blood flowed to the ground that day at Calvary, God's purposeful and intentional plan was victorious over more than sin and death; but every part of the Curse. A deliberate God gathered every thread on that horrible and glorious day, reclaimed it and knit it into the New Covenant.

Out of one man, Adam, sin entered into God's creation. Out of one man, Christ Jesus, sin and death were reclaimed and redeemed. It could not have happened any other way. God's holiness required justice – that the price of sin demanded payment - but His mercy provided the Lamb that would atone for sin; redeeming for eternity each one who would enter into His provision by confessing Jesus Christ as Lord and Savior. Only God could offer a sacrifice worthy enough to satisfy such a weighty account.

Confronting the Real Enemy

"Or how can anyone enter the strong man's house and carry off his property, unless he first binds the strong man? And then he will plunder his house." (Matthew 12:29)

Some people enjoy a good scrap. I am not counted among them. Where some seem to be exhilarated by intense, even heated discussion, driving home a point or insisting on the argument of their *right,* I would be in full retreat and looking for a way out. I did not learn to do confrontation well but did learn early to be very inventive with how to avoid it. Anger and dissension, even if not directed at me, would undo my inner peace, leaving me frantic to restore it. It was once said of me that I would confess to just about anything to make the anger stop. A bit of a stretch, perhaps; but point taken. It's a weakness that has threatened to make me as vulnerable to sin as the one who rages in anger.

To live in an extreme means, we live with an open door and are sure to become the prey of any force that exists beyond our ability to control it. To leave any door open in our soul is the same as living with a robber in our house; one who will require the balance of our peace and spiritual authority, leaving us open to the demands of a wily foe. Most who live this way struggle to maintain stability out of pure desperation, finding themselves given to anxiety over the seeming lack of control over those reoccurring pattern that keeps peace at bay with too much regularity. Anytime the same thing keeps popping up to undercut our peace, joy, or spiritual balance; we should probably conclude we are living with a door left open in our soul – one the shed Blood of Christ paid the price to close. If we are willing to roll it over onto Him and give our self to the process of deliverance from what has, by now, become a habit in our reactions, He is well able for all it takes to free our soul.

Some of these doors were jerked open by our hand; attitudes, habits, sin we dabbled with until some of them dabbled back and caught us. Some are doors opened by generations before us; ones we accepted unchallenged because it was just the way our family thought and acted. Most of us are left standing on the brink of our own life with a false view of who we are and the potential that lays just beneath the shrouded concept we now carry of ourselves and our future. It is a fearsome thing to consider that it was a false reality that created the lie we now live by; one that we are now responsible to either adopt or refute. An unexamined life is a great help to the enemy of our soul, the devil, whose mission it is that we would willingly accept our *fate* and never find out the Truth. To voluntarily live with the lie of personal or generational destruction seems a questionable choice when Christ died to redeem that curse from you and close every door, no matter who left it open.

My own dreaded conflict lay hidden for a long time. Having talents, abilities, a quick tongue and sincere heart, I found it easy enough to float on top of a river of sludge that most people never saw, or were kind enough not to mention if they did see. The battle began, not because of what others might have noticed, but what I began to see – in me. One cannot give oneself to Christ, to walk in His ways, and remain neutral about the areas of our life and soul that remain unredeemed. It didn't take a very big flash of revelation for me to know I had an open door that caused me anxiety on a regular basis. When faced with anger, I would most often swallow saying what I knew to be true for the sake of restoring peace. Not able to handle control or anger, I would become a shadow, and the real me would just flit away. It's no way to live, and the Holy Spirit's revelation will not allow it – for long. Sometimes we must confront the real enemy – and often that is our own soul, our willingness to live with something – anything - that robs from us any bit of God's redemptive provision. It's a process and most effective when done with kindness, compassion, and honesty, to be sure – but no one can continue to live in a house divided against itself (see Matthew 12:25).

I do not live there anymore, although it seems I am still invited, at times, to visit that old way. Revelation may show the seat of our bondage, but deliverance requires our cooperation – and practice, lots of practice – to learn to walk in a new way. Prayer was only the beginning; from there I've had to learn how to walk in my new-found liberty. Most times my flesh still wants to hide from anger and confrontation. There is no safety in hiding, it just feels familiar. But, God is helping me maintain this Truth revealed in and to me. And, although I still avoid conflict if I can find another honest way, I can meet it when I must – and not from a position of fear.

Into the Night

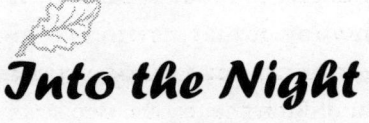

"For the Mighty One has done great things for me; and Holy is His Name. And His mercy is upon generation after generation toward those who fear Him." (Luke 1:49, 50)

Many days made up the journey from the manger to the Cross. The path was laid, its beginnings dimly lit by the star whose light came to rest above a stable in the hills of Bethlehem. Messiah was born; the journey to Redemption had begun.

Mary could not have been more surprised, perplexed that she had found favor, even more so because the message flew in the face of all that made up the flesh – she was a virgin. And yet, her response was, "…may it be done to me according to your word." (Luke 1:38)

Joseph, an honorable man with a pregnant fiancée, planned to put her away secretly, avoiding accusations; but a dream from the Lord was sufficient to turn him from the pride that the flesh so often demands and set his feet to the path of a higher calling.

If one of us were to imagine ourselves in a situation even remotely similar to that of Mary or Joseph, or the other main players in this story of the birth of Redemption, I think it rare we would see ourselves doing so without fear, doubt, second-guessing and uncertainty. Scripture never hides the humanness of Mankind, just glories in the workings of God there in the midst of them.

Now, Zacharias was a priest in the Temple and probably the most theological of this small group of humans through which the door of eternity would swing open. Knowing the most **about** God did not necessarily keep him from having questions, even giving fuel to them. When Gabriel recounted the details of the answer which was coming to his long-awaited prayer, Zacharias said, "…How will I know for certain?" (See Luke 1:18). At that moment he was struck dumb and would not speak again until the fulfillment of that which the Angel of the Lord had prophesied. Perhaps this was Gabriel's way of saying he needed to do more listening to God and less talking about Him.

Elizabeth was a righteous woman, blameless and now old, but she was childless. I wonder at the surprised joy that rose within her at the words she was able to whisper, confirming the promised son to her now silent husband.

Mary could not have seen the Cross when she crooned comfort into His tiny face or when she swaddled this Lamb of God. She knew only in part, but was faithful to what the present moment required of her. She had begun her journey saying, "…may it be done to me according to your word…" (Luke 1:38) How many days would she utter these same words before the fulfillment of the Promise, the one that made the mountains quake, the sky grow dark, and the veil between God and man was at long last torn asunder?

Joseph could not have imagined them nail-pierced and bloodied; those small hands he held in his own, the tiny fingers that, no doubt, curled around his work-hardened members. His own strong hands laid the child in his mother's lap as she sat atop the donkey that would carry them to Egypt. He was a man acquainted with dreams, the angel of the Lord confirming through them both the divine conception that had taken place within Mary and now God's unerring provision against the rage of evil that was being leveled by Herod against the Seed of the Righteous, "...to destroy Him." (Matthew 2:13) They were ordinary people called to do extraordinary things.

Each one God called and used in these pages of Redemption's Story was human in that they all had hopes, plans, and feelings. But, not a one allowed their flesh to dictate over the wisdom and the voice of the Holy Spirit, with whom each one of them was personally acquainted, recognizing Him as He spoke to them of things to come. They were all human and yet each one had been called by God to a divine appointment. We might hope to think so, but we cannot consider ourselves as different from them, or our calling less than theirs. In ways large and small we too are called to our part in bringing the birth of Christ into our daily lives, our conversations, our neighborhood, work, and school and church. The sound of that donkey's hoof beats still echo its message of Messiah throughout the Judean hills, to Egypt and Nazareth, to Calvary and the uttermost parts of the world.

On the Front Line

"For anger does not achieve the righteousness of God." (James 1:20)

We live in a world that is ever more inclined toward rage. It's a problem we recognize, but few know how to handle when it rears its ugly head in our arena of life. Rarely would a person given to tantrums say that division, strife or hurt was the outcome he/she was looking for when a situation gets out of control between individuals. Anger is usually an outward expression of inward frustration, or a desire to maintain control where one senses they have lost or are about to lose it.

I think most would say the world moves too fast; there's too much change, governments at odds, factions among people, too many agendas that few are inclined to trust or with which they agree. Add that to a rise in busyness where families work to provide more but have less time to know and enjoy each other and stress becomes a barometer that measures the point at which it will boil over in our relational or home lives.

No relationship is devoid of temptation or opportunity to go over the line into anger. Usually, if one has something on their mind, however small, they are initially looking for an audience, hoping to feel heard or understood as they press their point. Trust is probably the most fragile crossroad in the peace of any relationship – that each can go away from a conversation feeling they have been heard by the other. If one - or both - parties press for an advantage, a peaceful and equitable solution is rare. Usually, someone gets angry, and anger is a dubious door on which to hinge the health of any relationship.

Anger does not work the righteousness of God. Neither does a confrontation that slips into the nether land of *emotions out of control* bring anyone to a change of heart or peaceful resolution. Anger closes ears, hearts, and minds; argues a *right* to opinions and feelings. Demanding and overbearing anger will usually push one of them to a place that seems to resemble compliance. In reality, they only appear to comply; the more likely scenario is that the one who seems to give up the fight, stuffs the emotion inward, where it lays in wait for the next occasion. The truth is not that one suddenly agrees with the clamor of the other, nor have they submitted to what has now become a tyrannical demand; they only look like it on the outside. No longer able to answer the anger, they just refuse to continue the struggle.

The more subtle and underlying destruction in this relationship is the probable break in the bond of respect, trust, and confidence. These are the foundational blocks of any relationship and, once broken, are hard - but not impossible - to restore. If you find yourself in such a dilemma, you'll need help beyond yourself to repair the breach. I think there is no more dangerous relational crossroad at which to dwell, one road leading to redemption and restoration - if you can and will - the other leading to a root of bitterness, which springs up and defiles many (see Hebrews 12:15). It is husband/wife and parent/child relationships who represent the most prominent targets. The devil knows if he hits a bullseye there, the whole family stands to tumble on the brink of disrepair.

If we find our self in a position of needing to be right, we are not – right, I mean. Whatever point we were driven to make has long since been swallowed up by whatever drives that need for us to be right, to be heard, to be in control at any cost. Surely the loss of peace, relationship, and answers to our prayers is too high a cost. We live in a day when every foundational block; that which is sacred, decent, kind, or eternal is under grave attack – the family is on the high priority list, parents on the front line. "God sets the solitary in families: He brings out those which are bound with chains: but the rebellious dwell in a dry land" (see Psalm 68:6).

In a world that deifies power and control, where frustration is a task-master that threatens to leak into our peace at every turn, we desperately need an earnest heart on which to lay our burden down. He stands ready to hear and to help. It will cost our flesh dearly, these habits and reactions so subtly practiced, but deliverance is a sweeter fruit than bondage. What do we have to lose except the chains with which we are bound?

Peter is quite pointed about the place both men and women play in a marriage relationship (see 1 Peter 3:1-7). After speaking to both, he concluded, "...as a fellow heir of the grace of life, so that your prayers will not be hindered" (1 Peter 3:7). God is the author and defender of the marriage/family relationship. His eye roves to and fro, seeking open doors that He may dwell within.

Patches on My Bucket

"...This I know, that God is for me...In God I have put my trust, I shall not be afraid. What can man do to me? For You have delivered my soul from death, indeed my feet from stumbling, so that I may walk before God in the light of the living." (Psalm 56:9b, 11, 13)

Now I have learned a thing or two as I've journeyed - not unscathed by life - to a more mature age. Experience should teach us a thing or two – if we are paying attention – for that is both the purpose and design of life.

I was raised on an Iowa farm by a mom and dad who stayed together, worked hard and did the best they knew how by each of four children. By my early adult years, I had come to an uncertain conclusion there must be something wrong with me. Life seemed too hard, answers too few. I took each life experience as it came, did the best I knew to do, resolving what I could, burying the rest as deep inside as I was able. No matter how deep I dug the hole, those things never did stay buried. With a stunning regularity that which I tried to hide and forget would surface and present its argument, reminding me once more to not forget *this hurt, that regret or those words*. Yes, emotions and memories have voices too, and they are not shy about expressing themselves.

I can now admit that I was tempted and often indulged in blaming my parents for my damaged being, damage which often expressed itself through specific emotional weaknesses which left me vulnerable to hurt, rejection and an inability to cope adequately with certain situations of life. The only way I can describe it is that when I needed to be strong, I would reach into my *emotional bucket* to gather strength and wisdom for the moment, and find there wasn't enough to meet the need. When there are unhealed memories, we may find ourselves prone to reliving the hurt that accompanied the words or actions. It's impossible to maintain a façade of "all is well" when you live with holes in your bucket!

I have learned restoration can be one of this life's most liberating designs if we dare to let it. It teaches us we need more than the resources that are our own if we are to live above, and more so, beyond the limitations of our flesh and the circumstances that life is sure to hold. No one escapes hurt or pain, loss or shame. We'll either learn to dig it out of our lives or be buried by it. My first *clue* came when I reached out to the Savior, and He took me in. I did not seek Him out as a *fix* for my life, had no idea He could or would fix me. I had no idea that *fix* would come as a part of the redemption package, but it did. Slowly and surely He began to reveal the holes in my bucket and to patch them so they'd never leak again. Some might think He'd make the bucket new, but I rather enjoy looking at my patches – I never want to forget that He healed me in so many places.

No human has the knowledge, insight or resources to give another human precisely what they need, when and in measure as they need it. An advantage held by a parent walking in the counsel of the Holy Spirit, however, is that they learn early to point their child to the Source. No one knows a child better than He who knit them in their mother's womb and breathed life into their nostrils. But, even these will have their own experiences, hurt and hardships – leading them to the need for a Savior. Perhaps Solomon was thinking similar thoughts when he penned, "Train up a child in the way he should go, even when he is old, he will not depart from it." (Proverbs 22:6) I have found that knowledge may come swiftly, but wisdom will often tarry.

There is no formula for perfect parenting, for even the wisest among us is a work in process. So, the only recourse is to plant liberally into the lives of those who have come into our care and then to water with great abandon. The life is in the Seed; wait for it – if He has planted it, abundance shall inevitably spring forth.

There is no measure of comfort higher than the Truth that one who once was lost has now been found. To be able to exchange life for LIFE; to finally put to rest the driving and insatiable need within and trade it for a consistent Source, one who makes provision without condemnation and speaks life to a withered soul. He confirms the assurance of all that lays beyond the lie that life had thus far endorsed – a life redeemed and rich with promise. In Christ we have entered the door that leads to home, and that deep part of us that so long has hungered has at last found provision and is, at last, satisfied.

Bloomed as a Rose

"His speech was smoother than butter, but his heart was war; his words were softer than oil, yet they were drawn swords." (Psalm 55:21)

I think there is probably no disappointment in life more significant than to learn that those to whom we had entrusted our hopes, dreams, confidences and fragile affections had sorely abused our trust or even used them against us.

I'm not sure where this man had come from or what experiences his life might have held; this one in whose heart is war. I wonder what voices he heard, what picture of people and relationships he viewed that caused him to form his meager view of others and set his sly mouth to deal out slander. From what sense of evil pride does he gather the innocent and serve them up as the fodder by which he seeks to elevate himself?

"When pride comes, then comes dishonor; but with the humble is wisdom." (Proverbs 11:2) Solomon names pride to be the culprit of many misdeeds. If one were to listen to the mantra of the world, they say to seek after personal rights and self-confidence, it is vital to set goals to work toward and visions to attain. I think godly wisdom would agree, as long as we remember the Source from whence they come. Could it be there is a fine line between confidence and arrogance; pride being the subtle ingredient that would throw us over the edge where wisdom would counsel restraint?

I once, long ago, trusted a confidence to a friend. It was important, life-changing - for me - and I shared it because I thought I could. From my limited understanding, I trusted and it turned out I had trusted unwisely. Sometimes smooth words and a seemingly sympathetic ear draw us to expose our heart to another when wisdom - if we'd had it - would have counseled otherwise. When my confidant exposed my fragile flaw, it did not go well for me. I experienced a significant loss, humiliation and definite changes in my willingness to share about myself. A trust door closed within me that did not re-open for a long time. When it finally did open it was born out of knowing I would only share a confidence from a position of wisdom and not out of a need to unburden my emotions. I learned to be frugal with sharing intimate details, being prayerfully selective to only share with a safe ear, discriminating in the search for wise counsel instead of giving myself the temporary relief that may come from emotional and verbal diarrhea. I provide an ear that holds the respect of another's life to the same degree of integrity.

I'm not exactly sure of the entire list of *why's* that have become integrated into a person who sets their heart toward war, nor the underlying source of the sly demeanor that would cause them to hide behind "speech that is smoother than butter." Perhaps deep hurts, bitterness, jealousy or insecurities have so damaged them of the sense of who they are that they live from the position of trying to deal out water from an empty well. Their soul too has an enemy who seeks to rob and kill. Hurts, betrayal, lack or loss are not the things we factor into our life goals, but when they happen, we must choose the place we will give them and what attitudes and actions we will take regarding them. The experiences of life will build you, or break you, and the attitude - the position - from which you meet them will choose which it will be. Everything we know talks to us, attends us, and each one is a seed which we will either plant in God toward redemption or put in our storehouse of personal regret; where it molds, unused but not forgotten. Those things we allow to remain unredeemed serve no purpose but to remind our pride of its failure and to slander our soul. It takes courage to repent of having carried something that was never ours to bear in the first place, but those whom the Son sets free are free indeed.

It was a good number of years before God revealed to me the truth of what I'm talking about here. Time has confirmed the power of the forgiveness I both received and gave away. Because I learned Truth, I have been set free to grow beyond the loss. My salvation has always been about so much more than my soul and its place in eternity. My journey in Christ has provided a purpose in which to dwell. He has made a place to develop gifts, talents, abilities, an astute and sound mind, sensitivity to the Spirit and people, a good understanding that the losses in life will stay an obstacle in my mind only as long as I allow them a place in which to dwell.

Redemption returned my lost portion to me long ago. Christ filled the vacuum that once lay in my soul, the one where loss once dwelled. He provided substance that filled my longing and satisfied every hurt, every failure, all pain, and humiliation. In Him, I have been completed and served a portion far above what I would have known otherwise. Planted in Him, my desert bloomed like a rose (see Isaiah 35:1). I planted my loss in Him, and He sowed the seeds of redemption, in turn, teaching me how to plant with great abandon. My harvest has been abundant!

A Flea in my Pajamas

"So if the Son makes you free, you will be free indeed. (John 8:36)

My husband and I are now of more mature years and have managed to allow a few compromises to sneak into our well-ordered and spiritually mature lives. Our daughter has been raised for many years, long gone from our home. We've replaced the need to care for someone with a four-legged fuzzy *child*. We might as well refer to her as "Your Majesty," for she manages to hold court over our lives without ever giving a single command. And a compromise we've made to accommodate her every whim? We've allowed her to sleep on the foot of our bed.

Now, its late Fall in Iowa, the time where outside critters seek a warmer existence. And the reason I know that is because one of them, a flea, had quite evidently made its way to our bed by way of her warm little body and had taken up residence in my pajamas. I was awakened suddenly from what had been a peaceful rest by a sensation that something was amiss in my world. The more I tried to ignore it, the more it became impossible to do so. How shameful to have a flea in one's pajamas! I finally faced the fact that this torment was of my own doing, repented of it and took myself to the bathroom for liberation. Speedily exorcised, I sent my little tormentor to his eternal reward. Deliverance is not a vague concept but a real hope to one who has a flea in their pajamas. But first, I had to *own* the situation. By that I mean that I had to acknowledge it was real, my own responsibility in it, that it was most certainly affecting the quality of my life and I had a choice to make as to whether I was willing to live with it or seek deliverance from it.

Life is a lot more serious than a flea in our pajamas. There are those among us who have experienced unspeakable things; things they have carried alone because they think them too shameful to tell. They yearn for a moment's peace and release – blessed release.

It is often likely that anyone so tormented by the past has also become quite accomplished at flight. By that I mean, trying to run from the pictures that play, the voices that speak. Or, if *flight* is not their preferred escape, they have probably become well acquainted with what I shall call *the grave-diggers syndrome*, trying to bury "it." Grave-diggers may become quite inventive in burying that which is dead – their problem being that "it" never stays buried for long. Their hope is for a moment of peace; but peace remains fleeting. Perhaps now is an excellent time to stop and own whatever it is that has you on the run!

When I talk about *owning* a situation that one had experienced, it does not always have to do with taking responsibility **for** something. Sometimes it does, if we've sinned against another, but sometimes the sin was against us, and that calls for a very different position of owning. Being set free from a life-altering experience must begin by honestly acknowledging what happened there and that it robbed something that had been ours; perhaps innocence, perhaps trust, but something essential was stolen. The accusation against one so used is that the loss seems forever gone, un-restorable, and un-redeemable. Rest is not a commodity easily found when the *flea* of memories torments our existence, reminding us of its presence and its loss. We are left with the choice to live with it, try to bury it, or seek deliverance, all of which seems to offer seemingly insurmountable odds.

One of the many things I appreciate about God is that neither time nor circumstances bind His hand to move and to deliver. He is the same yesterday, today and forever. The sinful choices of free will have stolen too many innocent moments. Because God loves us, knows our every breath and paid the price to redeem each stolen moment, it would be an eternal regret to leave the gift unopened because we felt too unworthy or ashamed to ask to receive it. Redemption goes deeper than rehearsing a moment or confessing its pain; it absolves - to free from guilt, blame, or their consequences - each stolen moment. Let the accusations that torment our soul, *talk to the hand*; the One whose crimson Blood ran freely, covering the cost of deliverance from what happened there.

"Therefore, confess your sins to one another, and pray for one another so that you may be healed. The effective prayer of a righteous man can accomplish much." (James 5:16) There are safe places, safe people who you can trust to hear you, bind the torment or the memories, the accusing thoughts and the voices that accompany them. Let those "saints in light" pray and agree that the Holy Spirit has delivered you, removed the stain and released you. Deliverance does not mean the accuser will never revisit your memories, but that you have a powerfully consistent answer when he does. He who the Son set free is free indeed (see John 8:36).

A Strong Man's House

"But no one can enter the strong man's house and plunder his property unless he first binds the strong man, and then he will plunder his house." (Mark 3:27)

I believe every one of us was born, by divine intent a completed person, three parts in 1: body, soul, and spirit. Jesus refers to us as a "strong man's house" so let's just consider our three parts as making up the one "house" of which He speaks in Mark 3:24-28. Let us assume that our house has many rooms; these representing our gifts, strengths, personality, authority, even our health and our emotions live in this house that is known by our name. He also refers to this body we call home, as a "temple." "Do you not know that you are a temple of God and that the Spirit of God dwells in you?" (1 Corinthians 3:16) What we are, or ever hope to be, has been carefully laid out, built, equipped and gifted with enough provision to meet every need; this He has given into our care, for a season.

Considering that we are in possession of so great a gift, it is unthinkable that we would give away what was ours, allow squatters to live in our house and plunder our property. We might say we would never do such a thing, but if we have given ourselves to a sin, we've rented it a room. It might be anger, gossip, strife, envy, sexual immorality; you get the idea. These things take up residence in our house and rob us of hopes, dreams, satisfaction, peace – they steal our God-given portion during those brief moments when we gave in to the demands of our flesh. We have begun to live in a house divided, and that house will not long be able to stand (see Mark 3:25). Anyone who will not answer the call to salvation in Christ will spend a lifetime signing over the deed to his *house,* with no hope of return.

Having signed over the title to any portion of the house in which we dwell, we no longer entirely own nor do we have complete control regarding its use. Slowly the house rules begin to change, and we realize we have become the renter in our own home. That we have done so out of ignorance does not make a difference. We are sunk! Or, are we? Remember that part about "…the Spirit of God dwells in you?" We have an advocate that wars on behalf of our *house* and He contests for our soul, desires to redeem it. He already paid for our house, and all that inhabits it when the Blood He willingly sacrificed poured down the Cross on Calvary's hill. If we will allow Him to enter those rooms we had unthinkingly given away, He will redeem them, one by one, as we confess we need His help and allow Him. Only those rooms we refuse Him entry remain at risk.

I grew up having very little knowledge of spiritual things, but even I knew about the devil. I didn't pay him much attention, nor give him credit for the seemingly unimportant sins of my life. I didn't even call it sin – those little lies, a little this or a little that. My ignorance masked the reality of my loss and, while I did not pay attention to it, the devil did. With each wrong choice, each seemingly small act or omission; I gave away a little piece of my integrity, my honesty, my purity, my innocence.

At 25 years of age, I opened my heart to Christ, asked Him to forgive me and save my soul. He did that; the salvation He provided settling the question of my eternity forever; but, what of my days on earth yet remaining? I may have been a new creation in Christ, but a lot of my flesh still didn't act like it; or - in some areas - even want to. And, what about all that *ground* I had ignorantly volunteered to another master? My free will had permitted him to dwell in my house; could it be that my own free will demanded I be the one to evict him, reclaim the ground I had willingly, even unwittingly, given over. Free will demands a choice as to which master we will serve. God gave us free will; He does not violate what He freely gives. That's why it is ever necessary to be intentional about reclaiming what we had given away and just as intentional about putting it under the care of Grace.

We believe in error if we think salvation just automatically purifies our flesh, mind, and soul; the process works in tandem. Those bents toward sin, weaknesses of our flesh and stumbling blocks we find to consistently reoccur, testify there is something we need to face about ourselves. If they live in any part of us, we are not our own. Because it was we who rented out the room, it is we who will speak the eviction notice - and Christ who serves it!

Don't be afraid; the Holy Spirit is your Revealer and your Helper. If you have a past that re-occurs, a pattern you can't seem to break, a nagging hurt, habit or tendency, there's more than a little chance that somewhere, sometime, your flesh opened the door to the stranger who plunders your house. Reclaim it by calling it what it is and praying, "The Holy Spirit has exposed you, and you cannot live in my house any longer. Leave now, in the Name of Jesus Christ. With His help, I close the door to you. Holy Spirit, I ask that You fill this empty place, guard it and remind me not to go there again. I pray this in the Name of and by the shed Blood of Jesus, Amen."

Revival Whispers My Name

"And My people who are called by My name humble themselves and pray and seek My face and turn from their wicked ways, then I will hear from heaven, will forgive their sin, and will heal their land." (2 Chronicles 7:14)

It seems a long time ago that my husband and I knelt at the altar of what was then a small neighborhood church. We had not considered church a priority when we purchased our first tiny two bedroom home nearby, but we have since learned that God often orchestrates events you had not regarded as prudent or necessary in your life. We had never heard of revival, would probably not have understood or cared if we had. The human condition, separated from God, is infinite in its arrogance; refusing to ask God to save him and he cannot save himself. We were intent on our jobs, home, friends, things, pleasure – and a child. She's why we tried that small neighborhood church, not because we would have identified ourselves as being needy. Having never heard of revival was only one of the things we didn't know. Thankfully, what we knew or did not know about God made not one whit of difference when the Holy Spirit of the Living God began to sweep across our heart and soul. He gently started to make us aware of the gaping hole that lay within us, and the futility of our driving need to stuff it full of – well, anything at hand.

We were among the first wave of a flood of people who found Christ as Savior in the days and years to follow. To say our lives were unexpectedly and radically transformed seems to use words that are, in reality, too small to convey what happened inside us. In the beginning, we were a bit undone, so sudden was this new purpose that had been so suddenly planted within; one our lives would soon learn to follow. All we knew was once we were dead but now alive. Living half a block out the back door of the church gave us an opportunity to show up just about any time the lights were on – and show up we did – for everything from mid-week prayer meeting to the janitor scrubbing floors. We also stopped by regularly on our evening walk to kneel at the altar and pour out our heart petitions to the Lord in prayer. I once asked my husband if he thought we were going to get *religious*. He answered, "We're going to do this all the way, or we're not going to do it at all." If praying, reading the Bible and going to church constitutes *religious*, we were a couple of lost causes – lost to the cause of Christ.

Anyone who has been part of the miracle flood of revival, lives ever after with that hunger in his heart, wanting, praying, waiting to see God move in kind, saving souls and reviving hope with a life-giving sweep of the Holy Spirit – the kind that changes lives and families forever. All religion and grasping ideologies become weak imposters in comparison with the move of His Spirit.

It's not a huge leap to figure out that humans are looking for something to ease the pain of living. Day by day we see and hear of those who seek in vain to fill the hole of their own overwhelming need. Drugs, divorce, violence, abortion, perversion, food, vice, alcohol, religions of the world, seemingly anything that gives some sense of significance or momentary relief – and a bit of salt and light is God's provision to stem the rising flood.

Only the one who knows what it is to be eternally *lost* and void of hope can truly appreciate being *found*. Like a firebrand that has been plucked from the burning, (see Amos 4:11) we knew only too well how close we had skated to destruction. We cannot afford to lose sight of that, or our heart and hands will grow too quickly idle. The Church does not exist so the saved by Grace can rest safely within its walls, exclusive in membership and cut off from the troubling cries and messy lives of humanity. Those of us who make up this body of believers need sinners as much as sinners need the Lord. Show me a church with no new converts who are finding salvation through the Blood of the Lamb, and I'll show you a dead or dying church. Oh, how we need new souls saved – so we might never forget.

Having begun my spiritual life on the cusp of a revival, I hold that a move of the Holy Spirit is the only hope for a world that races toward destruction, and that it should happen first within His church, those people who are called by His Name. I've often pondered which comes first: do people call upon God for revival or does He call upon people to pray for it? Either one asks for a heart that is tuned to the need for the souls of men to find Him.

When Jesus told Nicodemus he must be born again, He also said, "The wind blows where it wishes and you hear the sound of it, but do not know where it comes from and where it is going; so is everyone who is born of the Spirit." (John 3:8) Perhaps prayer is God's people standing in the wind that always blows across the ears of those who would listen unto the whisper of His call.

Links in His Chain

"Now faith is the assurance of things hoped for, the conviction of things not seen." (Hebrews 11:1)

I know this verse, quote it to myself and the Lord often; but I'd be remiss if I said I wholly understand it. Sometimes I do, seeming for brief moments to rise to a level of revelation and understanding, only to fall away to the place where I know it's true, just not exactly why or how it works. Faith is a mystery to me most of the time. For a reasonably intelligent person, you'd think I'd be better at it. Perhaps that's because it's not a matter of intelligence; but about asking, accepting and believing without needing to know why or how.

Now "substance" is described by Webster as, the real or essential part of anything. Well, I guess that, while it seems quite profound, doesn't help me much. So, bear with me as I seek to sort through this. I'm going to try breaking it down into something a little closer to my life – something to which I relate. Hopefully, you'll find yourself in there somewhere. Most likely each one of us is praying for a loved one to find salvation through Jesus Christ. I don't know about you, but it sometimes seems the harder I pray the faster they run in the other direction. If that is an accurate reality, why then would we continue to pray? Well, Peter says, "The Lord is not slow about His Promise, as some count slowness, but is patient toward you, not wishing for any to perish but for all to come to repentance." (2 Peter 3:9) Now, that scripture becomes a substance we can hang our faith-hat on, for it speaks to the real and essential part of our prayer. It is not based on what we want or what we think, but on what God has said. We can safely plant our seed of faith in that because the outcome doesn't count on our failing flesh or inept ability. When we can confirm our prayer in His Word that is sufficient evidence that our agreement is with God concerning those things for which we ask. I can hope in that.

Sometimes we want or need substance to translate into provision, something we can hold in our hand or with which we can pay our bills. While it is true that God promised to meet all of our needs according to His riches in glory in Christ Jesus (see Philippians 4:19) let us be careful to temper our expectations with regard to what we *need*. When I read the whole of chapter 11 of Hebrews, I am struck by the distinct possibility that when we make faith only about us, our wants, needs, hopes, and dreams, we relegate that which is eternal to a place where only the temporary exists – earthly needs. I don't intend to diminish the need to pray for what we need; that is important as well. I would, however, suggest it is wise that we not limit our prayers. Let prayer speak to that which is temporary in light of that which is eternal. The Lord's Prayer is an excellent example.

As I read about the people of Hebrews 11, I cannot imagine that any one of them understood what the end-result of their "by faith" moments might look. Abel just gave the best he had, Enoch just loved God and Noah built, Abraham moved, Sarah laughed; Jacob wrestled, and so on. They would never see or completely understand what their part in the whole plan might look like, they just gave themselves to living out their faith, and planting to a harvest that lay beyond what they would hold or eat. It is likely that they had no greater sense of their part in the eternal than you or I, but they received their part by faith and carried it forth to the next generation with a faithful - although imperfect - heart. The eternal plan of God is first born in the heart of everyday godly people and realized in the world because the hands and heart of those same people willingly took the bag He handed them and scattered the seed that was in it. Where we view in part, He sees the whole, but we are the links in His eternal chain.

We don't often think about it, but nothing we see or hold has a permanence that will last beyond a few fleeting moments. And while it seems we talk a lot about purpose, it is rare that we acknowledge it in the everyday moments that are common to our life. Probably Rahab didn't consider hiding spies as having eternal value; yet there she is, listed among those who carried the faith, her name listed in the genealogy of Jesus. So let us continue to plant into and pray for loved ones; let us bless our church and our pastor, teach our children and speak of Him to those with whom we share our lives. What if….? It is no small thing when we are "faithful in the little things," (see Luke 16:10) when we are faithful to pray, rejoice, give praise and touch a life. Only He knows each link that completes eternity.

I confess that eternity is rarely foremost in my mind when I remind the Lord, "Now faith is the assurance of things hoped for, the conviction of things not seen." (Hebrews 11:1) So, I think it best to include the end of the faith chapter in my prayerful consideration, for it concludes, "And all these, having gained approval through their faith, did not receive what was promised, because God had provided something better for us…" (Hebrews 11:39, 40a) Amen!

Nothing Predictable

"And He said to him, 'You shall love the Lord your God with all your heart and with all your soul, and with all your mind. This is the great and foremost commandment. The second is like it, you shall love your neighbor as yourself.'" (Matthew 22:37-39)

When we are born, I think our soul within arrives upon this earth completed, free and without restriction. Up to this point, in most instances, we had been completely safe, our every need met without demand. Into the world, we came, with a loud squall of despair at the loss of our safe and warm habitation. Quickly that for which we were perfectly fit took over, we breathed our air and for the first time felt a sense of freedom. Our spirit was content in knowing that we had begun the journey toward all that had been written upon our soul by the finger of God, the potential our life would hold, all we would be and do. We were swaddled and coddled, finding most of our insistent demands for food and comfort swiftly met. We did not know about rules and restrictions, but we would learn of them soon enough.

Most of us got to learn about life's *rules* from the rationale that they were for our good; being told the rules kept us safe, helped us navigate the conventions of society in ways that were acceptable. It was an unspoken rule that any display of personal liberty was an inconvenience and behavior would be tolerated only within the firmly established parameter of acceptable rules. We soon learned that if one broke the *rules,* retribution was swift and close at hand. There were a few who dared to break acceptable convention, but they were subsequently clucked at by an authority figure first and then by peers. They insisted we get back in line and don't rock the boat. Although most secretly admired the courage of the one who flew free for a moment, the security of keeping the rules intact always won out, and even those who took to flight were soon brought to bear - or isolated – for *rules* demand that they are followed by all the good little soldiers.

It has been impressed on us often enough that rules keep us safe. I do see wisdom and need for specific regulations and would not advocate anarchy or that we eradicate the laws of society. These standards give us an expected path to follow, empowers us with a sense of control. Rules keep things predictable; establish a parameter by which men may operate within expected boundaries. But, they do not give birth to righteousness. A list of rules may strive to make us all look, act and respond the same way, may even evoke a sense of somewhat superior safety; but we are not saved and made whole by the list of rules that is Law.

When Jesus was born, the people of Israel had long perfected the rules by which they lived; they most commonly referred to it as, *the Law.* On Mount Sinai, God had handed Moses a list of Ten Commandments and a variety of ordinances that governed people, property, and behavior (see Exodus 20-23). By the time Jesus was born, there were 613 - yes, 613 - rules about how the original 10 were to be kept by the people, and the consequence if they were not. What God had established as a standard by which one may safely build a godly life; men had amended to a collection of laws. And, when the authority of Jesus challenged the rules of the religious order of the day, their response was to find a way to get rid of Him.

Rules do not – cannot - work righteousness in the heart of man. The Ten Commandments soon exposed man's inability to achieve the fulfillment of, even the essence of, the Law in and by himself. Those who spent a lifetime piously and religiously attending to the letter the Law were not only zealous; they had grown into legalistic and judgmental fanatics. And yet, as careful as they were to live in perfect accordance with the letter of the law, they did not recognize the Son of God who walked among them. Jesus did not fit the mold of what religious men expected. Part of their problem with Jesus is that He never made spiritual life about the keeping of rules. After He told them he had not come to change the law but to fulfill it He said, "'And you shall love the Lord your God with all your heart, and with all your soul, and with all your mind, and with all your strength.' The second is this, 'You shall love your neighbor as yourself.' There is no other commandment greater than these." (Mark 12:30, 31)

There is nothing predictable about a life planted in Christ and led by the Holy Spirit of the Living God. Discerning the voice of the Holy Spirit and interpreting God's Word is individual and personal to every man. Since He has promised He will not leave nor forsake us, His wisdom and counsel not only close at hand, they are essential to our spiritual growth and well-being.

A Peaceful Habitation

"And the work of righteousness will be peace, and the service of righteousness, quietness, and confidence forever. Then my people will live in a peaceful habitation, and in secure dwellings and in undisturbed resting places." (Isaiah 32:17, 18)

Where we live is not a significant consideration but how we live should be of great importance to us. Today I'm thinking of the importance of dwelling in "...a peaceful habitation." And, that has a lot more to do with what resides on the inside of our walls than the address on the doorpost.

Peace is an elusive quality in the world today. Nations at war, governments embroiled in controversy, hatred, intolerance, schools at risk, families in strife and divorce; the devastated world cries for peace, but there is none. There seems to be little we can do to avoid its threat and sorrow. If we are to hope for respite and peace we must begin where we live, I think.

Throughout Scripture, oil is a symbol of the Holy Spirit. When one was set aside as unto the Lord, it was with oil that he was anointed and thus dedicated to the Lord. It is never the element that holds power to commit, change or keep. The power comes from the covenant between the One who makes the invitation and the one who answers it; when an inner call meets Him who can bring it into being. It also affirms we agree with and choose to cooperate with whatever it requires to bring it about in us. Oil signed the Old Covenant; the Blood of Jesus signed the New Covenant. I took a little detour, but an important one, I think. I wanted to affirm what a simple bottle of oil represents to us and why we find it prudent to identify with and to use.

We are entirely serious about the concept of dwelling in a place where peace reigns. To help us stay in tune with the Holy Spirit, by practice, we keep a bottle of oil handy. Olive oil works fine. We pray and acknowledge it is a symbol of the Holy Spirit, saying by its use that we seek His help, counsel and covering. As often as we feel the need, we take our bottle of oil and begin by anointing the doorposts of our home, praying that God will cleanse, cover, keep and show Himself to all who dwell therein (see Exodus 40:9). Sometimes we do likewise in each room of our home; either acknowledging His presence resides there or praying if something comes to our mind. We don't make it long or complicated; it doesn't have to be. After our house, we walk the perimeter of our property; binding the influence of enemy, releasing the power of the Holy Spirit to lead us in all of our ways, to keep us from all harm and ever alert to His voice. We anoint with oil, by doing so we acknowledge it is His help we seek, entering into a form of covenant, I suppose. One that agrees: Lord, as You will lead, we will follow.

Anointing with oil is not like waving a magic wand, once done, promises to bring a happy ending, story over. Entering into an intentional agreement with Him who knows us and loves us will challenge our most deeply held concepts, change us, rebuke us, question our motives, our methods, and create within us a new heart. The more we encourage His Presence to dwell with us, the more we are encouraged to grow within an atmosphere of love and acceptance, without condemnation. No one can - for long - pray for a "peaceful habitation" and continue to war. The concepts are so completely incompatible that one must give way to the other. The only way peace can reign is that maintaining it becomes more important than being *right*, enough so that we lay down our weapons of war. God has laid down some compelling requirements for maintaining healthy, growing and nurturing relationships. We need to get it right with those with whom we dwell in the day to day if we are ever to expect to have a voice in our city and around the world. Home is our practice field and the seat of our strength.

By the anointing of oil and the laying on of hands, we agree we are set aside to His purpose. By it, we acknowledge His help to lead, guide, and cover and keep us in the process. It does not mean we are faultless in our commitment to Him nor in our commitment to live within specific constraints. Oh my, we are so less than perfect; but sincere in our pursuit of Him, none the less. And so, we renew it as often as we feel the need for we often fail and need to be reminded and revived. <u>We do not own each other, do not need to rule or control to feel empowered or of value</u>. Because we are complete in Him as individuals, we already have those things. Living in that kind of liberty frees us to enjoy our quirky individualism, gaining strength and contentment from our "peaceful habitation."

Where Doubt Once Lived

"And Jesus said to Him, 'If You can? All things are possible to him who believes.' Immediately the boy's father cried out and said, 'I do believe; help my unbelief.'" (Mark 9:23, 24)

It is a beautiful morning out my window today. Spring is making itself known, overcoming the hold of winter; all things are being made new. I can rejoice in that, confident in God's not so subtle reminder that no matter the coming and going of humanity's frantic shenanigans or their personal opinions concerning everything - even the weather - the world is ordered at His command.

It comforts me, this changing of the seasons. I find my heart lifted; my spirit encouraged at this reminder of God's Divine Order and the principles He has established; the One that keeps the world on its axis and the stars in the sky, the One who calls me by name. He who orders the seasons of my life does so with the same surety as the spring that swallows winter's tenacious grasp. I do not think winter mourns her passing, perhaps even rejoices that she has served the purpose God asked of her.

We can be confident that whatever life may hold at the moment, it is but a prelude to the next. How tightly we grasp the moments that pass too quickly; each fleeting instant now forever woven into the fabric of our lives, moments that changed the whole of it. We are people of change and process, one season laying the foundation for the one that will surely follow. That life is ever-changing cannot be disputed. What then might be the ingredient that causes one person to struggle and resist change, while others sail through the seasons and challenges of life with a bump and a skid, shouting, "Glory Hallelujah!" all the way? Is it an attitude they have chosen, this courage with which they seemingly face life? Or, is there an underlying ingredient?

All of life demands that we live by faith, and one way or another, we do respond. Thinking of faith in a negative context seems incongruent with God's intent for it. If we expect the worst, faith does her job and brings it to us; it goes into action according to how our outer expression -words and actions - matches our internal concepts - the truth of how we think and feel. No matter what our mouth might declare, if it goes against the grain of our inner beliefs, we are just spitting words in the wind. If we privately view ourselves as a victim or unworthy, if we are stubborn and hard-hearted, living in doubt or fear, this too is living by faith; only in reverse, bringing to our life the very things we say we don't want.

Perhaps we hope it will work the other way around; that if we say it long enough, we will begin to believe it. Faith, being the ingredient upon which all of our life balances, is born from the inside out, the author and perfecter of it being the Christ who dwells within our being by the power of the Holy Spirit (see Hebrews 12:2). It's not unusual to have a season in which we struggle to have confidence that He hears our prayers, seasons when we find it exceedingly trying to be aware of anything other than personal thoughts and unanswered questions. It's a standard in a growing life; a call to question what we believe, measuring whether our faith lays a foundation upon which we may safely build a spiritual *house* or an uncertain platform of doubts. Unbelief is what eventually happens when we will not challenge our thinking and conclusions;

it encourages beliefs that remain unquestioned or unresolved, applauds spiritual laziness and apathy as well. Unbelief also delights in discouragement and despair, and invites us to dwell there.

A faith that is healthy challenges and roots out those thoughts and actions that cause our heart to be discouraged with too much regularity. Once challenged and revealed, it becomes increasingly important to fill that empty place where doubt once lived with the Christ that dwells within; by prayer, study in the Word of God, and keeping our life accountable to safe, mature believers who understand faith and live by its principle. God has always had a plan for our life, one for welfare and not calamity (see Jeremiah 29:11). If we were to listen to the voice of the Holy Spirit within our being, He would tell us of that plan there written upon our innermost being; the prophecy whose price had been paid in full by the shed Blood of Jesus Christ before we had drawn a breath. Redemption is the process through which we first become aware of the debt Christ has already paid. Once redeemed, we may then begin to reclaim what He had intended as our portion from the beginning – and faith is the ingredient which causes this feeble heart of flesh to look to the Promise of God and receive the inheritance He set in store for each of us.

Still Practicing

"Not that I speak from want, for I have learned to be content in whatever circumstances I am." (Philippians 4:11)

I've been thinking about the Apostle Paul and his decision toward being content, no matter what life held or threw at him. To be honest, I have an easier time doing that with the parts of my life that I can keep in some semblance of control. Doesn't sound very spiritual, does it? I looked up the word *control* in my concordance. Should it come as a surprise that the word control does not exist among the many thousands of scriptural references there listed? That makes me wonder if it is perhaps unimportant to God that we have, it, or keep it, or use it. I pondered control from God's point of view toward His Creation but got as far as free will and had to deduce that although God could have kept it, He chose to give choices into our keeping. He put the Earth and the animals under the care and dominion of man. That shows a measure of trust in Man for which we've not always been grateful nor responsible.

Finding nothing about control, I did, however, find quite a bit regarding the word *bondage* and some words derived from that concept. It made me wonder if the notion of control is more about us - our desire to feel like we have it or fear that we are losing it, or living under it. Then too, if God didn't address it in His Word, might it be the theory only exists in the flesh nature of man, a tool of destruction in the hands of an unseen foe? The devil does use our flesh against us. Tempting us to live by its demands, he seems relentless to control our soul through bondage here on earth – the incessant hate, discrimination, and mayhem that rages at the wily suggestion of the one who was cast from the heavens to earth along with a third of the heavenly host. Lucifer, Satan, Death, the Devil – you know, the one Christ defeated and stripped of power at the Cross! For a defeated foe, he sure seems intent on taking as much with him as we unwitting and often lazy humans will give into his dominion – and control.

Which brings me again to my thoughts on control and how little – none - of it I have about those for whom I care, the sometimes bad choices they make, those resulting in confusion, loss, pain and the destruction that often accompanies those decisions once made. Because I'm a *fixer* and a *doer*, my first go-to response is to do something. Most people's first reaction would be to let me. It rarely changes the person or the situation, probably giving only me a momentary respite from the pressure I feel when there is seemingly no one at the helm of their life. It doesn't exact any sense of lasting change or restoration, only prolongs the problem for another day. Perhaps control says more about the person who needs to use it than the problem it seeks to fix.

I'm practicing - key word for me, practicing - rolling the person, problem and my own need to help, over onto God. I do know that control is the illegitimate child of fear, but I often find myself wrestling with what may lay at *the bottom of the barrel* that some seem so intent on finding. It's not easy to watch life exact its full measure before their knee is finally bent before a God that sees the heart and struggles of us both. The truth of my conflict lies deeper - in my ability to trust God with those I love. If I give way to fear, I become as helpless as they. I can do nothing about it but pray; that I can do! I can also refuse to let my mind go where disappointment lives. Faith in times of trouble remembers His Promises, speaks them in the face of this present reality and binds the power that rejoices in this moment. I can roll them onto the Lord who knows their innermost being and has promised He would never leave them or forsake them. If I can't trust the circumstances of their choices, then I shall plant my trust in Him who has promised.

So, I'm practicing: practicing keeping my faith that God's Promises, long-held, have already written a Truth that has yet to be made known. I'm practicing how I can love them without judging their actions, encourage without controlling and help without fixing. It challenges my flesh, but I think I'll keep on practicing until I get it right. Knowing what is Truth, even believing it, does not make it real in one's life. We are all accountable to live in Truth - that's what makes what we *know* become what we *believe*. So, I'll be content to practice what part God would have for me until the day comes when all things to work together for good.

Faithful to Redeem

"Therefore there is now no condemnation for those who are in Christ Jesus." (Romans 8:1)

Few reach the age of maturity without a past and, when faced with it, there is little we can do to sufficiently answer the charge the voice of our past lays against us. We cannot change it, apologize enough, rewrite or forget it. The choices we have made, the people we have hurt or wronged, deserve an answer from us. If we will not answer them, or think we cannot, it is a debt that remains unpaid. It seems some of the hardest words to say are, "I was wrong." But, when it is true of us, they are also the most liberating. There are some things of which we are truly guilty and those need to be made right to the best of our ability. If we have hurt another, stolen their property, their good name or reputation, asking God's forgiveness is not enough; we need to make restitution (see Leviticus 6:4-7). Please remember that our priest is Jesus Christ. Restitution means to restore something taken away, making good for loss or damage. It is an important spiritual principle, especially if we seek to rid our soul of the voice of guilt and condemnation. Of some things we were guilty and, while asking forgiveness of God and man removed the stain of sin, our flesh needs to make amends or, sometimes, pay the penalty.

I was a church secretary for 28 years in my earlier days. I remember a young man who came to our church offices for counsel one day after accepting Christ as His Savior. Being smart and good-looking hadn't kept him from making some unwise choices, and the consequence that now faced him was a trial and the potential of some serious prison time. His hope in the whole thing was that since Christ had forgiven him of his sin, absolution from the penalty of it should follow – and he was right in a spiritual sense – but man's law did not recognize salvation as an appropriate restitution, and he did go to prison. Although few of us will face jail for those things we've done in the flesh, I think we all have a similar hope that those confessed sins that slipped into the forgetfulness of God would do the same before man. Some do, but not all.

It is true that Christ forgives every offense we confess to Him. But, there is an element of sin that, although forgiven of the debt of it, we are not released from the responsibility of it; not until we have done all we can to restore - make good on - what we took away from the person against whom we had sinned. There is a subtle distinction between condemnation and conviction.

Condemnation produces guilt, which leads to destruction; it tears down our confidence, rendering us unsure and exposed.

Conviction creates awareness which aims us to the restoration and purpose Christ laid in the plan for Redemption. It is the eye of God that searches out the open doors of accusation in our soul. It answers to the higher law of integrity which compels us to face the charge with honesty and the authority to make it right to the best of our ability – or perhaps His ability acting through us is more accurate. Because conviction serves as the eye of God, it searches out the open doors of accusation in our soul and makes a way to answer its voice for all eternity. Work the plan and find the peace.

I'm sure there are some instances where it is impossible to restore what we robbed from another. In those cases, all we can do is repent, for the deed, for the fact we did not attend to it when we could. There's also a subtle distinction between guilt and guilty. At times, guilty is an emotion we need to hear. When it is true of us, we find power over its indictment when we face it and acknowledge the responsibility of what we did; then we lay it on the Cross of Jesus Christ and proceed to make it right. It is in God's nature and His provision that we have all we need to live above the accusation and condemnation the voice of the enemy of our soul (Satan) would lay to our charge. It is also His nature and provision that we do not presume upon His Grace and ignore whatever seed of truth the accusation might hold. If it's true of us - past or present - then it is a door left open in our soul. God wants very much to close those doors in our life that keep us vulnerable to the voice of the enemy's accusation. It is vital that we can answer what may have been the truth of us with the knowledge that the debt has been paid in full and has no claim on our soul, our testimony or our peace.

The path of righteousness is sure, and He is not willing that any should perish in unacknowledged pitfalls along the way. The Truth of "...no condemnation..." rests in Jesus Christ, for He is the One who is faithful to redeem us, not in part, but the whole of us.

Searching for a Millstone

"Whoever causes one of these little ones who believe to stumble, it would be better for him if, with a heavy millstone hung about his neck, he had been cast into the sea." (Mark 9:42)

When we were children and headed out the door to school or play, my Mom would often say, "Stay out of trouble." We were not particularly prone to getting into trouble, but you don't always have to look for trouble for it seems to have a way of looking for you. I think it has not been any different since Eve decided she would like to try that apple – and everything changed.

I wonder if Eve admonished Cain and Abel to stay out of trouble the day they went out to sacrifice. The day Cain decided to give God less than his best and ended up offended because Abel gave his best and God honored his sacrifice above Cain's. I don't know that Cain woke up that morning and purposed in his heart to find trouble but the opportunity arose and he did not turn away. To become offended was the open door, an opportunity toward evil and he walked right through it, thereby changing the balance of the rest of his life – and to his generations to follow.

According to Webster, this is the archaic definition of offense: *a cause or occasion of sin, a stumbling block*. Perhaps the most authentic interpretation of the word is that unresolved; the one will lead to the other.

At some point, each of us will have the opportunity to offend or be offended. No matter how carefully we guard our flesh, sometimes our tongue gets ahead of our brain, and we find ourselves offering an unkind word or - more likely - a hastily expressed opinion that hurts the one on whose ears it falls. It may have lacked premeditation, was never our intent to be so careless but there we are: guilty of an offense.

Although our greatest strength lies in diversity, it also seems to be the bumpiest road relationships walk. We are just so very different; and while we might find that interesting, it doesn't necessarily leave us with a foundation to understand why *they* do, say or act the way they do. We will never completely understand each other; and having different values, motives, history, or culture lends itself to the opportunity to be offended. But, there's certainly a bigger plan at work than momentary hurt feelings. At times the smallest seeds that one takes to heart and nurtures there can efficiently divide and isolate individuals to the position of outrage. Unresolved, those involved will soon begin to dance around each other instead of with each other.

Because peace in relationships, churches, and nations always produces more value than strife, it is an evil plan that keeps the unity found in peaceful relations at bay; a commodity ever hoped for but rarely realized. To be offended means that for a moment, sometimes a lifetime, we are off-ended. There are varying contexts and many roots, I'm sure, but it's not unusual that judgment or jealousy hide somewhere beneath the hub-bub. If either lies within our own heart toward another, we will find it impossible to keep it to ourselves. Eventually, an occasion will arise, and our opinion springs forth on a tongue of lightly veiled arrogance and offense is a likely result. We may try to *pretty up* the words, give 16 reasons why we are *right*, we may even throw in scripture or two; but if judgment lays beneath our motive, the offense should have just become the least of our concerns. Thinking one's self to be *right* is a slippery slope to stand on. Perhaps this might be a good time to begin the search for a millstone (see Mark 9:42).

The reasons for offense, once entered, quickly cease to matter. Everyone gets off-ended on occasion so it becomes more of a matter of what we will do with it when it happens. To remain standing on a platform of an offense changes the position and balance of our faith. We don't like to look at it as sin, but I'm not sure what else to call it. Appearing to His disciples after the Crucifixion, Jesus "… breathed on them and said, 'Receive the Holy Spirit. If you forgive anyone his sins, they are forgiven; if you do not forgive them, they are not forgiven,'" (see John 20:22, 23). He was not telling them they had the power to forgive sin, but choices; let it go or hold on.

There is only one answer to offense: you are the keeper of the door through which deliverance lies. If the opportunity comes to be offended, and the craftiness of our flesh will make sure it does, someone has to say, "Enough." Earlier is better for each time the opportunity for offense comes; it comes better prepared for its argument of right. The Lord can never bring deliverance until someone dares to rip up the records that offense has kept; and that cannot happen unless we engage our will to let it go and, thereby, agree with the power that works in us.

When we are Old

"Train up a child in the way he should go, even when he is old he will not depart from it. (Proverbs 22:6)

It is a remarkable responsibility, a significant challenge of life, to train up a child in the way he/she should go. It will require more wisdom than we have at our command and, indeed, insist on a sense of balance that hangs between order and liberty, holiness and tolerance, obedience and willingness toward sacrifice. Whether it is our physical or spiritual child, we will need the same sense of consistency and responsibility, one that requires that we have embraced Truth and steadfastly live our lives in equal measure with that which we expect of another – children in particular.

There is an old adage that says, "Do as I say, not as I do." In reality, these words pale in the light of the great need that we live as a standard for those who would look to us as an example of how to live, how to act, react, speak and honorably conduct themselves in the day-to-day. The goal of training is never that we might turn out miniature versions ourselves, rather to encourage each one under our influence and care with the awareness and courage to become who they were meant to be, to know how to live out of the provision and resources that God planted within them. That's not always so easy – especially if we are uncertain as to whom we are, what we believe. We cannot sow liberally out of an empty *sack*, cannot give what we do not have. We cannot ask another to live according to what we do not fully believe and do not live. The message our children take with them into their lives will be the message we have lived before them.

We began sending our only child to Sunday school when she was 5 – *sending* being quite telling regarding our lack of personal beliefs and spiritual mindset. It said we knew the importance of spiritual teaching but were too lazy or too cowardly to lead the way. That didn't last too long, our lives drastically changing after I got saved while volunteering to help in Bible school. My husband soon followed, and the atmosphere of our home began to know transformation, in ways large and small. We began to pray before our meals, had Bible stories, discussion, and prayer before bed. God – loving Him, serving Him and the church - became our *normal* in life. We had found Christ, and we were forever changed, by choice. When God moves supernaturally, His Spirit sweeps many to know and walk with revived hearts and lives. Our family was part of such a harvest. We lived for Christ and revival became our way of life.

That must be the end of our story, right? Everything was automatically smooth sailing, with a perfect outcome, right? Well, yes but no! We had an outrageous amount of baggage we had brought with us to this new life and so very much to learn. We had experienced the gift of salvation, but we were also unchurched and unlearned. We were not lazy; we had fallen in love with the Savior, so accepted that redemption was a process; one that we gave ourselves to with everything we had! We made multitudes of mistakes. Thankfully, one of the first things we learned was that it was not about us – how perfect or imperfect our walk and our habits, how much or how little we knew, how correct our behavior or beliefs or how often we failed. One learning to walk in the ways of Christ will have a lot of new beginnings and, if they're wise, they will soon learn to rejoice in every one. Each failure, each new beginning was never hidden in our home. It seemed important that we model that repentance was an essential part of the Christian walk, significant enough that we'd better stay familiar with it. As much as possible, we made our lives – at home, work, church and social – transparent and about Christ, His Blood, His Word, His redemption and His Promise. It's not how good at parenting we were that holds our child, our seed. It is not our perfection that will continue to call them and keep them when they are grown and growing old – it is the Life we modeled before them in the moments, in the day-by-day, of the lives we lived for Him.

Our daughter has made her way, has known hard times and much heartache. She has struggled and made her mistakes. She also has the sweetest spirit, is cheerful, stable and consistent, loving Christ, planting her seeds of love and acceptance, her prayers into the imperfect situations that life is sure to hold for every generation, hers and the ones that now follow.

Faith does not confirm a perfect life, the day nor hour of our deliverance or the moment of an answer to our deepest and most heartfelt prayers. It just reinforces and affirms that He has heard and will answer at the moment of His choosing and has given us the strength, resiliency, wisdom, and courage to carry the promise until the season of its fulfillment. Generation to generation, He has enabled us to claim that when they are old they will not depart from it.

A Plan for a People

"Every place on which the sole of your foot treads, I have given it to you, just as I spoke to Moses." (Joshua 1:3)

I wonder what conflict arose within the heart of Moses after he defied his assumed heritage in the palace of Pharaoh and killed the Egyptian who was beating his Hebrew brethren (see Exodus 2). He could have turned his face and walked away, but he did not; but then, perhaps the day of his purpose had come and he could not. Ill-prepared to be a deliverer of anything, even Moses considered himself unlearned, unprepared and unable for that which the Lord God would ask of him. For every opportunity where deliverance was needed, God prepared a man or woman who was perfectly fit for the occasion; but nowhere in Scripture have I ever found that when God called a deliverer He then just left them alone to figure out what they would need to know or do to fulfill His call. The circumstances of the life of Moses do not necessarily fit what might seem appropriate for a deliverer. He had murdered a man and then ran to avoid the consequences. Only God can know the depth of man's sin and call him anyway. God had seen the suffering of His people and their day of deliverance was at hand (see Exodus 3:7-10). Moses would be His mouth, His hands, and His feet. I appreciate and somehow identify with Moses's human-ness, his curiosity at the bush that burned, his honesty about his lack and eventual obedience to God's compelling call. I think even if had Moses stayed in Egypt, the bush still would have burned before him. The day of deliverance was at hand!

The people of Israel knew nothing but bondage; slavery held nothing more than distant imaginings of a path that might someday, somehow lead to deliverance. Do you think they dreamed of or prayed for a land in which they might know peace or liberty? "So I have come down to deliver them…and bring them to a good and spacious land, to a land flowing with milk and honey…" (Exodus 3:8). Oh, and by the way, there will be challenges and enemies you will have to subdue - my paraphrase, His message.

Plagues, escape, the Red Sea, Ten Commandments, obedience, disobedience and 40 years of wandering in the wilderness later and Moses was not able to enter the land that God had shown him. There's a lot that makes up the story as to why, but perhaps that which is most telling about the godly man Moses had become through the wilderness-process showed up in the attitude of his response. If he was disappointed, he did not speak of it; instead, he blessed the people, reminding them of all God had spoken to their forefathers. They were not the generation that received the promise; they were, however, the generation who would fulfill it. Perhaps it is always that way; to some God speaks the Promise, to some the fulfillment is made known. Moses did not bless their preparedness, their understanding, their courage or abilities; he spoke of what God had given into their care for the days ahead of them. The Promise was always about the One who had spoken it and the plan of Redemption set before the people who had been called to act on it.

Scripture should always cause us to consider what message it speaks to our own life. Every one of us has the privilege - and I think the responsibility - to claim God's Promises for our personal lives and our generations. To do so is a part of our inheritance in Him, allowing the purpose of all we hope for to stand on something more substantial than our resources. As with Moses, when we claim His Word for our own life, our family and future generations, we will always be faced with a choice. Do we run to speak blessing upon the seed planted within us? Or, do we allow life's disappointments to rob the plan because the burden of it was too much to carry, or it didn't happen when or as we thought it should? Perseverance is measured to our account when we faithfully bear what God had promised, for each generation is called to walk out their specific part of its fulfillment. "...I will make you the repairer of the breach, the restorer of **paths to dwell in**," (see Isaiah 58:12 KJV). He spoke those words as a specific invitation to pick up the Promise because someone had laid it down. Our prayer should be, "Oh Lord, let it not be my generation who lays down what You have given into our care."

Let us carry what He has given, and do so with the assurance that it is ultimately He who keeps it, fulfills it and prepares our hand for whatever challenges it will require of us. Moses blessed the people who would inhabit the land, content in the knowledge he had been faithful to his part. His life was measured not according to where his feet had taken him - or not taken him - but by his obedience to God's eternal purpose within the path his faith had walked!

"...I will be with you; I will not fail you or forsake you. Be strong and courageous for you shall give this people possession of the land which I swore to their fathers to give them." (Joshua 1:5b, 6)

I Didn't Do So Well

"For in the way you judge, you will be judged; and by your standard of measure, it will be measured to you. Why do you look at the speck that is in your brothers' eye, but do not notice the log that is in your own eye?" (Matthew 7:2, 3)

The phone just rang – again. It does that multiple times these days, with various schemes or solicitations. That we are in a hotly debated presidential election doesn't help. People with opinions, loyalties to something they may or may not completely understand or agree with urging someone, anyone, to pledge their allegiance to a cause by way of rehearsed rhetoric and unsubscribed agenda. They all want you to do something, believe something or buy something. Her name was Tara, and I'm sorry Tara, but the calls get wearisome.

I didn't do so well. Being a part of God's family here on earth, I could have at least been kinder. I was not, as I rudely interrupted her, letting her know her one of a dozen or so calls I would receive today was not appreciated. My answering machine is not rude; I probably should have let Tara talk to her. I can be a real creep, and the Lord's gentle voice within me convicted my heart! My response was far less than gracious, and there's no place for that if we genuinely believe the Words of Jesus regarding our behavior.

Guess I still have a long way to go to kindly live out these Truths and revelations about which I like to ponder and write.

I think today I will ponder how I, having been saved from so much and blessed with so much, can still be such a creep and so quickly run to ungodly judgments. I judged Tara harshly. Without knowing one thing about her, my unkind response inferred a conclusion on her job and her person because she was doing it. Judging is like that – sneaky, riddled with a haughty arrogance that would presume the whole of something or someone, gauged on the small window through which it was viewed. That this was just a telephone solicitation and not *real life* does not dismiss my responsibility for a Christ-like response of basic courtesy and integrity administered with kindness.

I have often wondered at the verse which follows immediately on heels of Christ's pointed challenge to judge oneself first. "Do not give what is holy to dogs, and do not throw your pearls before swine, or they will trample them under their feet, and turn and tear you to pieces." (Matthew 7:6) I think these statements are not unrelated. Instead, a pointed reference to the danger we pose to our soul when we open the door to a more significant evil through the petty purposes, attitudes, and actions that flow from the heart of every judgment and everyone who judges. An open door, even the smallest-seeming crack, leaves us vulnerable to an enemy whose purpose is single-minded: to keep us so busy with flesh, emotions, and opinions that we will never discover the power and authority given to everyone who names the Name of Jesus Christ.

In a world that boils with ever-growing evil, we stand well prepared with resources that enable us to meet every situation that presents itself. Christ said we would do greater things than He (see John 14:12). God, the Father, gave Adam dominion over all the earth but to Christ, He gave all authority of heaven and earth (see Matthew

28:18). And, because the same spirit that raised Christ from the dead dwells in us (see Romans 8:11), we are meant to live life from that position of authority to pray and claim in His Name, to rebuke the devil, to speak life and faith into seemingly impossible situations - and into the smallest moments as well, Tara.

I think most who name the Name of Jesus Christ understand our authority on some level but often find our prayers without the power that brings about a change or an end. Perhaps it would be wise to consider whether it could be our judgments and opinions that might be a stumbling block to the answers we seek. It is not unusual, having already determined our expectation of what the answer will look like, having already decided the eventual outcome about that which we are praying, that we find ourselves telling God what we think and what we have concluded. What we feel, think or expect has no place in faith, no place in authority and cannot be misconstrued, even remotely, as agreeing with His Word – which is our only hope for an eternal answer. It would be well to remember to pray God's Word in our prayers, to stay in agreement with what He says about things; to remain under the mantle of authority of His Word. Our prayers are mostly regarding things that have captured our attention and our heart. Let us then intentionally keep them about what He says and not what we think, thereby, increasing the opportunity to rejoice in their answer.

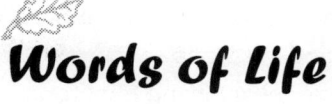

Words of Life

"For as many as are the promises of God, in Him they are yes; therefore also through Him is our Amen to the glory of God through us." (2 Corinthians 1:20)

If you have given yourself this far to the reading of my words and thoughts - and by the way, thank you - you probably have noticed I talk a lot about myself; things I've learned, challenges I've faced, some I struggle with and hopefully some I've overcome. I guess my life is the only experience I have, the single person I genuinely know both inside and out. I hope you don't find me a little too honest; all the challenges reflected in these pages should probably label me a questionable source but writing about what I've learned and am still learning helps me - and hopefully you as well - to think about life and God; and perhaps experience Him from a different perspective. I guess my most candid and revealing thoughts probably come from my pencil. And so, for today, I'm thinking about the Promises of God.

I learned about the Promises of God early in my Christian walk. I don't remember that anyone explained about claiming God's Promises, it was just faithfully done and frequently rehearsed! The people in the church were just everyday folks who worked jobs and raised families. What made for a unique distinction were their Bibles and their conduct with regard to it; the well-worn, well read and marked pages, their conversation and lives riddled with its words, its precepts and its blessings. That they might have considered the Bible just another book would have been unthinkable. It was their guide to life and godliness; written to reveal the nature of God, what Jesus accomplished and the life and inheritance He had laid up for us if we would live within His precepts – or what we could expect if we would not. If they considered it a book of "do's and don'ts" I cannot remember anyone ever referring to it in that manner, nor do I ever remember being taken aside and chastised for how little I knew or how short my newly saved life must have fallen from the light of their wisdom.

In their care, I learned that, although a man had written the words, they were inspired to do so by the Holy Spirit. It was not a historical account, but intimately personal words laid down on paper, written to countless generations yet unborn, awaiting revelation, spoken to any man/woman that would take it to their heart and live within its pages. It does give help, counsel, guidance and some "do's and don'ts" designed to keep life in balance, productive and eternal; but I learned to follow in a clear and well-worn path as it became to me so very much more. It became My Book, allowing me to claim the words written there for my hopes, dreams, family, and future. Now I am one who writes in it, underlines it and plants within its pages my greatest desires and most persistent longings – and often, my failings. It challenges me as I find real people there, their hopes and dreams, their problems and sometimes their frailty and sin. It has become my real hope, my comfort, my challenge and my revelation.

The Promises of God are not absolutes which, once claimed, go on automatic pilot to turn out an assembly line of believers who walk, talk, and act the same. A Promise is offered to us by God's Grace; it does not mold itself to us but allows that we might be molded to Him through the power of the Holy Spirit. When mere words on a Bible page suddenly appear to be explicitly written to us, giving inspiration and enlightenment, this is the beginning of revelation. If we take time to ponder them, they serve to shed light on specific areas of need or questions we be-labor in life. We begin to think about change, are challenged to live and walk in a more honest and balanced way; are inspired to try something new or stop something old. Revelation is vast and varied, personal and speaks to every man/woman with a different voice.

It is naïve of us to think we would avoid being challenged by what we read there, what it says to us or requires of us. Voices of condemnation, doubt or scorn too, will accompany the challenge to change, arguing it to be foolishness with the lie that it's safer to stay the same. It's up to us to determine if we will give place to the shadow that doubt and condemnation casts.

The shed Blood of Jesus Christ made all the promises "yea and amen" to us. He fulfilled His part, sat down at the right hand of God and opened the door for us to walk in what He has completed. Our role must surely be that we would walk within its charge and according to His purpose; which requires that we not only know what His Promises say but that we take them as our own and live as though they were Words of Life; for that is what they were meant to be.

Called to a Higher Level

"So that you will walk in a manner worthy of the Lord, to please Him in all respects, bearing fruit in every good work and increasing the knowledge of God." (Colossians 1:10)

Many would probably agree they used to think things got easier with age and experience. Sorry, only the nature of the battles changes as one grows older. Discouragement and weariness grow voices that argue of unanswered prayers, long-awaited, and ridicule our prayerful care. The urge to be cynical or critical awaits the opportunity to express opinions regarding the world and the ways of man; not willing to admit that judgments might only be a loosely woven distraction to hide one's discouragement, unredeemed failings, and unanswered hope. Oh, what a battle of temptation we face when we begin to long for those days, now past. Days when life seemed easier and we more wise and carefree; naïve days, when life had not touched our hope, and all possibilities lay tendered in the fertile soil of faith that was, as yet, untried. Knowing the Truth does not make it easier to walk in it, and memory has a way of rewriting the past.

It matters not the age or experience of God's people. All are called to think, act and believe at a higher level, an eternal purpose, learning to walk as one worthy of the Blood He shed to redeem their soul, to forgive when wronged, love one's enemies, bless those who hurt you, give cheerfully and deny yourself. These all a high calling, and ones that require forthright honesty, earnest repentance, resiliency, diligent courage, and faith in an unwavering Source beyond human ability or resource.

And yet, Christians are often criticized for being weak, intolerant or narrow-minded; often accused or portrayed as judgmental simpletons who need a crutch to limp forth upon an uncertain path. I realize that some who name the Christ as Savior could be guilty as charged, but that brush paints strokes too broad and colors too pale to be true of all, or even most. It does, perhaps, show just how skewed any viewpoint can become when any one of us seek to condemn the whole by what we see through the knothole by which we choose to view. Most often criticism is an opinion based on a small seed of truth and a whole lot of assumption, twisted to fit the point one is trying to make.

Most of God's people know all too well the failings of our human condition. That is most likely what made them seek the change offered within salvation in the first place. They know if it were it not that the Holy Spirit is a patient and long-suffering Teacher, long on forgiveness, it would be an impossible task to teach one's failing and tattered flesh to live above the reality presented in the world. Christians are not ignorant of the challenge life holds, nor surprised when society demands they live with integrity in the light of the *human condition*. It is not too much to ask that the world holds God's people to a higher standard. If not we, then who – "… for everyone who has been given much, much will be required…" (Luke 12:48) It is perhaps easier to list the ills of the world than solve them. Scripture says things will continue to get worse before they get better, that fine day when Christ splits the Eastern sky and returns to claim His final victory. Values will continue to lessen. Humans will continue to demand they be allowed to believe their self-devised version of truth according to what they believe truth to be. Respect will remain a morsel to be withheld or bestowed according to the opinion of a miserly heart and factions will argue their *rights* supersede personal responsibility and remain so without consequence.

And, in the face of that world, the people who call Jesus Christ, Lord, are called to be salt and light. I think that salt does not argue with decay, ask to be vindicated, or have an opinion on death. It merely does what salt does: it preserves and gives flavor where needed. And light? Light does not consider the power of darkness, nor call it an enemy to wrestle into submission by mind or might. Light just illumines! Perhaps that's what makes darkness so mad.

I conclude that being called to a higher level, to put into action the scriptural Truths, principles, and choices outlined in the Gospel requires more than a heart that is discouraged and faith that is feeble. Trust is faith in action, its confidence resting in the knowledge that God has made a provision for every occasion – EVERY OCCASION – and will make all things work together for good, as He said (see Romans 8:28). His Word is the only armor one has against the argument our *times* will make.

He Who Owns it All

"Blessed is the man who trusts in the Lord and whose trust is the Lord. For he will be like a tree planted by the water, that extends its roots by a stream and will not fear when the heat comes; but its leaves will be green and it will not be anxious in a year of drought nor cease to yield fruit." (Jeremiah 17:7, 8)

In an American world where our stores, homes, garages, and attics are overloaded with *stuff*, it seems we should have plenty that promotes contentment; yet that is more often only a veil that lightly covers the truth of us. As a nation, we have known only brief periods of history where abundance was not the rule of the day; as each subsequent generation seems to require, and have, more than the previous. Continually our government grows larger, our economy in greater debt, while the greed and lack of responsibility for present choices are pushed down the road, putting future generations in a genuine form of servitude. Politicians talk of providing ever-increasing benefits, accomplishing it at the expense of personal liberties and higher taxes. Everyone seems to have an agenda which only serves to feed the machinery that rolls on and on; often seeming to view those they promised to serve with lightly veiled contempt; they spout vain platitudes that promise, somehow, the end will be different than the course set before us. It is tempting, in the midst of so much plenty, to dismiss the overwhelming needs that have accompanied it and quite tempting to "Americanize" God, often viewing our priorities as His own.

I suppose it easy enough for those familiar with the Old Testament to leave the children of Israel to their seasons of bondage, thinking they earned their punishment by their own disobedient choices. Israel was always chasing after other gods. I don't remember that one was named, "avarice," that greedy devil that accumulates more and more, his hunger never satisfied; but I do remember one whose name appears regularly throughout Israel's history: Molech, a pagan god, to whom a proper sacrifice was your child. That God didn't look kindly upon the practice was an understatement; "Then I myself will set My face against the man *(woman),* against his family...their people..." (see Leviticus 20:2-5). It seems a precarious perch to live in the shadow of such disregard for the life of a child; peculiar to desire so much, continue to ask for a blessing when daily the lives of children hang in the balance between life and death.

Only God's hand can reverse such a swell of blood, and our part in it must be that we are honest with ourselves, use our voice, make prayer a priority and support those righteous people whom God has called and placed in a position to change laws. It is not only the rogues who bomb, burn or murder that has aligned themselves with the deed they seek to avenge. Says the Lord, "Vengeance is Mine, and retribution, in due time their foot will slip; for the day of their calamity is near, and the impending things are hastening upon them." (Deuteronomy 32:35)

The future did not bode well for Israel when they turned their face from God. We sometimes forget that at the height of their season of wealth and blessing, they too were the most powerful nation on earth. We do so much that is so right; but we should not stick our head in the sand, thinking that God somehow overlooks our sin because of our good intentions. He scattered His chosen people to the winds of the world in 70 A.D. and Israel as a nation ceased to exist until it again came to be in 1948, but we'll save that story for another day.

Watching the world that threatens to spin out of control will, I think, bring out the best and worst of Mankind. Some will set their hand to the plow to pray and do what they can, while others rant, giving place to the violence that rules an inner rage. Looking for someone to blame, politics and politicians become the target of their discontent, never stopping to consider that those who serve us are but a mirror that vaguely reflects the society they represent.

When Man chooses to live according to his own choices, without restraint, the best of them is left wanting, leaving those who hope in God the only hope we have left. Though the days before us prove a scary ride, it is not the time to hang our heads and idle our hands as ones who have no hope. It was never His design that pain or plenty would drive the choices of man, nor in the midst of either; the heart would live like a pauper. We are called to be that tree of which Jeremiah speaks, the one planted by the water, that extends its roots by the stream and does not fear when the heat comes, will not be anxious in the year of drought, nor cease to yield its fruit.

God is still in control so let us rest in Him and do what our hand can do: pray, trust Him and use the resources and gifts He has put in our care. Small choices, prayerfully made, moves mountains.

Subject to the Truth

"See how great a forest is set aflame by such a small fire? And the tongue is a fire…" (James 3:5, 6a)

It's not always easy to keep our opinions - which so often cover that sneaky thing called judgment - to ourselves. We somehow think we are entitled to our carefully crafted cover but, if so, we must base it on something more substantial than what we think or feel.

We might call what we believe, the *truth*. But, the qualifier of *truth* must ultimately be the *Truth*. How the one stands up to the light of the other should make all the difference when making life decisions, choices or the attitudes we maintain and so freely speak. One stands on the Word of God; infallible, unchanging; the other on what we currently know - or think we know - subject to our experience and interpretation, which will change as we grow in both. That's one of the reasons we need to hold each other loosely when we consider individual beliefs we - or another - may currently speak or keep. We - or they - may be on a journey to someplace new and trying to figure things out. When there is much to learn, it takes time for us to realize that what we know is only in part. Let's give each other some time to work things out and not be so quick to squelch what might become a new revelation to them - perhaps us as well - if given some time.

I have a few people in my life that have some pretty far-out beliefs about God and spiritual things. I don't always see things the same way, and although they have thus far been too kind to verbalize it, they no doubt wonder about some of the things I think about as well. If we're seeking and growing spiritually, our mind should continuously be filled new ideas, revelations, and thoughts; challenging us to concepts, visions, and places we've never been before. If that is true of us, however, it then becomes increasingly important that we don't just swallow everything that comes down the pike but resolve to keep our truth subject to the Truth. Ask the questions: Is this a new revelation? Does it give an opportunity for others - ourselves included - to grow in hope, does it encourage change, does it increase us in spiritual stature? Does it honor and line up with the whole of His Word? Is it only based on some vague scripture taken out of context? If not verified in Scripture, we need to scrap it. If so, then we need to give it some more time to *cook* if we are to understand what He's saying to us and how He wants to complete it in our lives. We must guard what we allow ourselves to conclude - about what we think upon and what we say.

There are certain Truth-principles God has set to live by in His world, principles that can always be counted on to work consistently in the same manner. They are neither for us nor against us. They just are, and work for our good or ill, according to how we apply them. Faith is one example, the law of sowing and reaping another.

James talks about the tongue being the smallest member, yet capable of setting great fires. Most of us have, at one time or another, experienced the heat of coals that little member has lain down and the pain of trying to apologize or explain away what we had said, humbly seeking a moment of redress or a way of escape. Oh yes, there is extraordinary power held in the tongue. God spoke the cosmos into existence; we do no less in our personal world. It is a sobering thought to be kept by such responsibility, held accountable by our own life for the words that issue with such regularity from our heart and roll so casually off our tongue.

We will not always have a choice about every circumstance that touches our lives, but we consistently have a choice regarding our beliefs, our reactions and the words we speak about them. No matter how good or bad a present circumstance of life may seem we will not live in that moment forever. We move on, the road on which we then travel paved by our own beliefs, our words, attitudes, and choices.

We've all had occasion to admire people who rise above adversity. I do not believe that happens by accident. The ability to do so was planted and practiced long before it was needed. If we are to live by faith in the midst of challenges, we do so because our heart-condition has been formed by the Word of Faith and our response to it long before the day of adversity arrived. Christ finished all and set it under our authority and care. We appropriate what He has done by first believing it, then practicing a position and attitude of faith. Our tongue speaks out of the belief that has been born and lives in our heart. We build our world out of that substance.

Free Indeed

"Then Peter came and said to Him, 'Lord, how often shall my brother sin against me and I forgive him? Up to seven times?' Jesus said to him, 'I do not say to you, up to seven times, but up to seventy times seven.'" (Matthew 18: 21, 22)

It is most unusual that any one of us grows to maturity and does so unscathed by the various hurts that seem to easily accompany life, especially those from our growing up years – those formative and impressionable years. We err if we believe those sweet bundles of budding humanity are without souls that hear and test every atmosphere, honing life responses and senses with which to gauge moods, everything and everyone that surrounds them. Always casting about to determine safety or danger, acceptance or uncertain disinterest, we listened, and were either satisfied that we were safe or our senses became instantly alert, on edge and watchful; for what we could not know. We as yet could not know it as lack nor could we think of it as damage that would affect our future days; we were simply gathering the information necessary for survival.

Most of what we experience in life was not intended to be destructive to our newly-budding inner self, nor was it usually imposed out of malicious design; not often. It was a response - or lack thereof - that rose out of each generation's individual and gaping hole of need, the things each family considered normal and passed from one generation to the next. That's how it goes, each generation having a significant effect on the one to follow; unending, or so it would seem. It is continual - unless there is a moment of great awakening that changes the soul, the life, and the pattern. The change that happens in a life redeemed never affects that one person alone; the liberating sense of redemption snatches us from the path of destruction we were doomed to repeat and opens a new way in which we, our future generations too, may now walk. Our first taste of the need to forgive usually comes with those with whom we have lived.

Few argue against the need for forgiveness or that we need to extend it to others. Most find it easier for us to be forgiven by God than for us to forgive another. God doesn't get caught up in the emotion of it and never keeps a list to refer to later. He forgives and then removes our sin as far as the east is from the west and remembers it no more (see Psalm 103:12).

We, however, often do get caught up in emotions. We do remember. Hurt is real, the feelings are real, and the wounding bleeds genuine emotions that are accompanied by pain and memories! In the face of this human reality, the most common hurdle in forgiving another is the fear that forgiveness somehow says that what happened was all right. Although we may not go so far as intentionally wishing pain on another, we might find ourselves looking for some form of vindication, some retribution that acknowledges the *guilty one* will also know pain – a payback of sorts. We forget that whatever we cannot let go is a cord that keeps us forever tied to that person, place and time. We are only accountable for what we do, not what another had done – unless our heart leans toward revenge. Wishing for retribution is the same as casting seeds in two separate fields, and hoping destruction will only grow in one of them.

Jesus spoke in very plain language when Peter asked him about forgiving; saying that our forgiveness is contingent upon our willingness to forgive others (see Matthew 18:21-35). To walk as one who has known forgiveness carries weighty responsibility for we are asked to forgive in turn – but up to seventy times seven? That seems almost beyond our ability to comprehend, let alone to live with such an open hand. But then, perhaps there are those offenses that touched us so profoundly that they will come to our heart and mind, again and again, seeking to regain their position of pain in us. Were we to pick it up once more and consider it in our heart, it will enter back into our soul, take up ownership and rule over our heart and emotions as though it had never left. Yes, there are those things that went that deep, and for those, we will need to live in a continual awareness of forgiveness; keeping the *torturers* at bay (see Matthew 18:34) because we keep our memories planted in Him who holds our heart and soul, seventy times seven. If that's what it takes to remain free, then so be it – seventy times seven.

Sometimes we're the guilty one. For us, forgiveness is the beginning of absolution, which means: to be set free from the consequence of guilt. Forgiveness says, "I release you." Absolution says, "I see nothing of consequence upon you." Since God cannot look upon sin, only the Blood of Jesus carries the power to cleanse sin so we can stand clean before Him – before man as well. Once redeemed He sees just the redemptive and cleaning flow of the Blood of His own Son and sacrificial Lamb, Jesus Christ, restoring us to those moments when our sins are forgiven and removed as far as the east is from the west, and He remembers it no more.

The Only Power We Have

"Therefore be patient, brethren until the coming of the Lord. The farmer waits for the precious produce of the soil, being patient about it, until it gets the early and late rain." (James 5:7)

It's quiet today in the early light of morning. No sun to greet the day, its brilliance hidden by gray clouds that sweep across the vast expanse of troubled sky. In the distance a low rumble of thunder gives promise of rain; much needed, for the earth is parched and in need of watering. So it is with my soul. Each morning as I arise I acknowledge the need for my soul to be refreshed by the Lord of all Creation. Before the hurried activities that will soon enough fill the day, a quiet moment for Him alone.

Today He reminds me that He has given much to my care, for He has given all men dominion over the earth. With authority comes a responsibility to care for, respect, nurture and enjoy. There is a delicate balance to nature, and He has charged man with the responsibility to keep it. I suppose some have used that authority to destroy because of ignorance or greed. Balance is a delicate commodity; if we are diligent to maintain its strength, we can know His provision to be sufficient, for the earth will abundantly meet the needs that man has for his existence. Even the beauty that first captures our awareness then refreshes those deep inner recesses, feeds the need of our soul to sit a moment in rest. These are the gifts He brings to everyone who would slow down long enough to let them touch us.

God has been abundant in His supply, creating a world that revolves around Divine Order and established principles. When man operates within them, their provision is abundance without limit; but to ignore them is to open the door to a destruction that knows no mercy. It may not come swiftly, but it will surely come. Although man must be aware of, and undoubtedly understand this on some level, I'm not sure what would cause one to greedily misuse the resources at hand as if there could not be an end to water, natural resources or fertile land. Could it be that man, if left to his own devices, might be so caught up in present moments of personal satisfaction, filling the gaping hole of need, that he would sacrifice his tomorrow to keep today's accusations and hopelessness at bay? If asked, would he say as Cain, "Am I my brother's keeper?"

We have become a generation of fatherless, often motherless children. Abandoning our responsibilities, even calling it our *right* to do so, is no less defiant or shocking than those who cast their children to the fires of Molech (see Jeremiah 7:31). Our generation has just chosen a slower road to destruction.

I rarely use quotes other than Scripture, but I'm going to include these words. They are pertinent to the days in which we now live and sound truth as well: "Human rights' are a fine thing, but how can we make ourselves sure that our rights do not expand at the expense of the rights of others. A society with unlimited rights is incapable of standing to adversity. If we do not wish to be ruled by a coercive authority, then each of us must rein himself in. A stable society is achieved not by balancing opposing forces but by conscious self-limitation: by the principle that we are always duty-bound to defer to the sense of moral justice." ...Aleksandr Solzhenitsyn

There is much in life over which we have no control. Since we have no control over the past, seeking His wisdom and help in making the choices that will form our future becomes the only power we have. Why would one not diligently exercise that choice? What are God's expectations for affairs and choices of every man/woman? Micah says: "He has told you, O man, what is good; and what does the Lord require of you but to do justice, to love kindness, and to walk humbly with your God?" (Micah 6:8). It seems we often tend to make things more difficult than it needs to be, I think.

Into our care has been given dominion – responsibility - for the affairs of earth and the needs are great. Our most significant burden, I think, is seeking God regarding His part and how that relates to what He asks of us. If He asks it of us, He equips us for it. No one has the resources to meet the whole of the need, but we can each supply a bit of it. I doubt that each raindrop felt personal responsibility for the Flood, but each contributed. Draw not back your hand from dealing out what you have to the needs you see before you; sow generously of the seed that is in your hand. This parched and needy world prayerfully burdens the heart of many this morning. We await the rain, the latter rain that the Holy Spirit of the Living God will send upon His Creation, reviving hearts and calling them to rise above the adversity of the moment to those things He has laid in store for us.

A Higher Priority

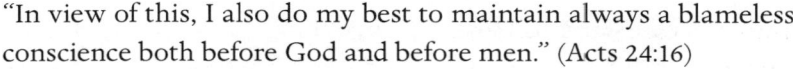

"In view of this, I also do my best to maintain always a blameless conscience both before God and before men." (Acts 24:16)

When written, this scripture found Paul standing before the governor, Felix, defending himself for being, "...a real pest..." (see Acts 24:5) to the Law and the accepted religious practices held by Jewish religious leaders of the day. His defense was (paraphrased) that, although they were different in their approach, they both believed in the Law and the Prophets, would one day stand resurrected before the same God. "In view of this, I also do my best to maintain a blameless conscience before God and before men." (Acts 24:15) Please read Acts 24:1-16, therein Paul was telling them that he was sorry if the way he conducted his life in the Lord offended their religious sensibilities but he answered to a higher authority.

I don't think so much has changed from Paul's day to this. In the USA we are not likely to be hauled before the governor to defend our faith – unless it conflicts with current health provider laws or statements of faith displayed on public property. We do see signs of the noose beginning to tighten on religious freedoms. In faraway places around the world, people of faith are putting their lives at risk for the sake of the Gospel of Christ and sometimes losing. It becomes ever more apparent that maintaining a blameless conscience before God and man is not always without risk. The world grows evermore thin-skinned and easier toward offense.

Offense: An injury or wrong done to one, a stumbling block or cause for temptation. I think at times the offense one feels is real. More often it exists only in the mind of one who cannot, or will not, accept the wide gap that exists when another is so diametrically different from us - and one, or both, is unwilling to move toward a bridge. I'm sure there are things we can do to change that, but for today let's stick a little closer to home and think about the offenses and misunderstandings that walk in our day-to-day lives, families, and friends. It's not so unusual that we will also find ourselves to be *diametrically different* within this arena as well.

It often seems easy enough to get our feelings hurt, and at some point, we will all find ourselves at that crossroad. At that point, the choices are: letting it go, addressing it, or carefully saving it in our little gunny sack of *feelings*, to be brought out at a later date. If we're a *saver* it doesn't matter what the original intent of the offense might have been; we will make our interpretation and use it to gain an advantage, to accuse, or to drive home our opinion or *rights* at some point down the road. At that point, the truth of the circumstance has ceased to matter. A *saver* collects tidbits to use to his/her advantage against another at some future and yet to be disclosed moment. That's where the term, "you always..." originated.

No one is exempt from the potential for offense. Whether we intend to do so or not, eventually we will say or do something to which another will take exception. We all have relationships and even when giving our best effort, it is not unusual for either party to see or hear perfectly imperfect. Being the target for an evil plan that is afoot in the world makes us vulnerable to an unseen force that is ever seeking to isolate husbands/wives, brothers/sisters, children/

parents, churches or governments; any bond where strength might lay.

An offense usually starts out small enough but, unresolved, won't stay that way; only waits for the next occasion so it can maintain the *right* of its existence. It is not unusual that one party remains completely unaware of what they said or did to cause such a rift. Give an offense enough time to fester, and it becomes a near impossibility to resolve. These offenses seem to collect innocent bystanders as they progress. As we engage others to our *cause*, they often become the collateral damage, drawn into a battle that was never their own.

There is no way to stop a cycle of offense but for someone to cease resistance. It would be nice if the guiltiest party would begin but it is usually the one most sensitive, the one most likely to count the cost of what they have to lose – or gain – by addressing what has become apparent. One merely chooses to step away, giving themselves to the higher priority of a *blameless conscience*. That may not immediately resolve the problem, but it changes the dynamics enough that it gives the Holy Spirit a chance to work a plan for resolution. It is a brave, fearless - and wise - person who sets aside their need for vindication to serve a higher priority.

Fanning the Flame

"For this reason, I remind you to kindle afresh the gift of God which is in you through the laying on of my hands. For God has not given us the spirit of timidity, but of power and love and discipline." (2 Timothy 1:6, 7)

Having grown up on a farm in the 40's and 50's, I have a special appreciation for Paul's analogy of fanning the flame. It was my Dad's job to coax fire from the embers that had held through the night in Mom's old cook stove, but all of us learned how to do it. Under his watchful care, we soon understood the procedure as well as the limitations and benefits. We learned by submitting ourselves to be taught by "the laying on of hands" (active, intentional commitment). My Dad first covered our inexperience until he could transfer the authority and we could fan our own flames. We were cautiously optimistic in the beginning, not because we were afraid to tackle something new, but because we respected the power and authority he was about to place in our hands. We needed first to submit to being taught, and then practice what we had learned until it became part of us.

Paul was undoubtedly fanning the flame of Jesus Christ as he traveled to places we know only by name: Corinth, Phillipi, and Ephesus. Since his experience often included being chased out of town by those who were offended or infuriated by the Gospel he preached, much of the ministry of shaping and teaching the newly converted, Paul put in the hands of men we know only through Paul: Barnabus, Titus, Timothy. They were the "keepers of the flame" that had been ignited under Paul's teaching, helping to settle church controversy but most often helping to establish new converts in the faith and keep their newly formed churches healthy. By the "...laying on of hands," they too were transferring the authority to these new converts who would soon have flames of their own to fan. Perhaps things have not changed so much. God is faithful to send those who will teach, encourage and equip those to whom the authority will soon fall; those who will hopefully go to their world and fan the flame.

The fire of the message they preached was raging across the known world, burning in the hearts of people who knew nothing but the idols of yesterday, the gods with many names. They still lived in the same fallen world, surrounded by the same idols and the same gods; but the faith in Jesus Christ that now resided in the hearts of these newly converted had the same potential as the ember once held - before a forest about to be consumed by flames. They would change the world, encouraged and shaped by the men whose words still speak from the pages of The Book. The need has not changed. Paul says, "No soldier in active service entangles himself in the affairs of everyday life... Consider what I say, for the Lord will give you understanding in everything." (2 Timothy 2:4a, 7) He was teaching Timothy the principles of good fire building, the authority and responsibility of it and Timothy, in turn, was teaching those who would set the world aflame.

These things I remember about starting a good fire:

(1) Start small (2) Lay a good foundation (3) Nurture the flame (4) Add to the fire slowly, being careful not to overwhelm it with too much fuel (5) Savor its light and warmth.

You'll know I'm old when I tell you I fondly remember standing before the old wood-burning cook stove that stood in my mom's kitchen with the name, Kalamazoo boldly emblazoned on the oven door. She fanned flames of her own in front of its sturdy frame. It was my brother's job to gather the corn cobs from the pile my dad kept in the corn crib, and my responsibility to fill the wood box. Perhaps that's why the fire felt so warm and comforting on a chilly morning when we raced to stand before it. We all had shared a part in its spreading warmth. Although my dad was the authority over the fires in the family, he considered it a commodity whose essential value lay in the transfer. He always led the way; he was the one who rose before we did, was consistent in the process, confident in the principles and believed in the outcome. He respected the fire, but he had faith in it. As we practiced, we began to recognize its potential and started to have faith in it too. I think Paul's hand upon Timothy, his teaching, his words, and encouragement did much the same.

Perhaps it's important to remember that the people who surround our lives, those with whom we share our days and those who we only touch in fleeting moments, remain just so much *kindling* unless they know the touch of a spark - one that hopes to become a consuming fire. Pass it on!

Let None Be Taken

"The kings came and fought; then fought the kings of Canaan at Taanach near the waters of Megiddo; they took no plunder in silver." (Judges 5:19)

I particularly appreciate the Old Testament and am captivated by the message within those books that establish God's Covenant with Man, the Promise of a land and all that went into making the Promise a reality. I like the honesty and the human-ness of the people on those pages, each one finding their way in the life God had called them to walk; and the struggles, I like the struggles. Not in the sense that I would have wished any of it upon them but because I find myself and my journey often reflected therein and am encouraged. Truth is always a revealer of our heart and our way if we can but allow it to be and to do so.

Now in that day, Israel's form of government was a Theocracy: meaning God led. The Judges were His chosen instrument to lead in battle, make prayerful decisions of policy and settle disputes that might arise. It worked very well, as long as the people submitted themselves to that God-ordained line of authority; the challenges to it very often came from the mixture that lived in the land. Yes, God had given them a land to dwell in, but Redemption never arrives completed; instead, it is a journey made up of the revelation and battles, victories and sometimes defeats that go into the process of taking possession of what God has given us. Had the land the children of Israel entered been empty, their story may have been different. But any mixture allowed to remain in any of our lives influences the whole; the existing values, priorities and goals often being at complete odds with those we are trying to establish. Allowing opposing concepts to dwell together was where Israel had fallen short. And the Lord said, "...I brought you up out of Egypt and led you to a land which I swore to your fathers; and I said, I will never break My covenant with you, and as for you, you shall make no covenant with the inhabitants of the land... But you have not obeyed me, what is this you have done?" (Judges 2:1b, 2)

This generation of Israel did reasonably well and, as long as Joshua was their leader, they served the Lord, even in the midst of the mixture - opposing influences - they had allowed to remain. But, Joshua died, his generation passed away, and the next generation paid the price for the formers' disobedience, for they began to serve Baal – the primary god of the mixed multitude. Stop a moment and let us consider what that might be saying about the life we are living in the here and now of today. It is sobering to think that our generations who follow might pay a terrible price because we had been nonchalant about sin. The very thing their fathers had regarded with casual attention, those things they had allowed to remain unchallenged and unchanged in that land the Lord had given into their care, undermined the way they practiced their faith and stole their children away from the Lord God.

I could not help but draw a distinct parallel to our own country and times. Truth has been battered, diminished, traded away and often outlawed from public display. It has been watered down to a feel-good absolution that tickles our ears and keeps us from feeling the weight or filthiness of our sin. Now we too are faced with a generation who often dismiss faith and the gravity of sin as they bury their awareness in the mixture of electronics, human rights, spiritual famine and a church that all too regularly lives like God is dead. Probably few of us have escaped its effect on a loved one and wonder where we went wrong.

Lest I leave you with hands that hand down or heart discouraged, let us stop and bless the remnant. God is not dead; He always has a shred that remains faithful – that portion that knows His voice and bears the righteous seed to the next generation. "In the same way then, there has also come to be at the present time a remnant according to God's gracious choice." (Romans 11:5) The momentary reality is that our world is a battleground, one which we can neither ignore nor avoid, for there is too much at stake. It is our feet that march forward to seek God, our knees that bend in prayer, our mouth that speaks His authority over the strong man, that blesses His Word and His plan; for He is not without one. Colossians says, "For by Him all things were created, both in the heavens and on earth, visible and invisible, whether thrones or dominions or rulers or authorities – all things have been created by Him and for Him." (Colossians 1:16) No matter how bad the world seems, no matter the inflammatory news or political rhetoric, He uses all things to perform His purpose and plan. Evil need not frighten the children of Promise; He has overcome the world. When we intercede in prayer, we stand in the gap between the need and God's supply.

I find comfort in the thought process and prayerful conclusion that accompanies this obscure verse in Judges 5:19 when the Israelite kings when out to meet the Canaanites there by the waters of Megiddo. Knowing that it is often our children, our generations that are the plunder of the enemy, the prince of this world: let none be taken! Amen!

A Work in Progress

"For I am confident of this very thing, that He who began a good work in you will perfect it until the day of Christ Jesus." (Philippians 1:6)

As one who is, too quickly it seems, growing to more mature years, I realize I wished away some of my richest moments. The young are so busy rushing from one task to another that often even those moments sitting in the sunshine are spent adding to their mental list of things to do. It seems easy enough to allow even the pursuit of pleasure to become a frantic task-master as if cramming one more activity into an already bulging day gives them permission to check off *the day had meaning* box.

Our daughter, now a grandma, could still remind us that she won every "Hi-Ho-Cherry-O" game we ever played – and why. She knew we let her win so we could finish the game and move on to other things. Those are the moments you mourn in more mature years because you know them to be lost to you forever because you wished them away.

Looking back, I know the essential things always got done: a job, bills paid, chores – and activities, lots of activities. But, I could not define one of them for you with poignant remembrance. What fills the treasure box of the more mature is the memory of a round little face looking up into yours, the sound of laughter, two bodies - one large, one small - laying on their stomach watching ants in the sunshine. It's either sunshine or regret that fills your heart with memories; regret being the harder burden to bear. We do have power over regret but only for today; waiting until tomorrow to change one thing is to lose what today might have held.

If we are paying attention, life is a fair and judicious teacher that presents many nuggets of truth for life and godliness for our consideration. Here are a few of mine:

- I am a work in progress
- Time is a gift – I will redeem it
- I will purpose to hear and heed what the Holy Spirit speaks to me about me
- I am not the Holy Spirit to the life of others; I will abstain from judgment
- Today is the window through which I view tomorrow; I will heed its counsel
- It's alright to feel emotion as long as emotions do not rule my choices
- Anger is acceptable only when I can keep from sin because of it
- I do not know about His plan for anyone but me
- When someone asks me for counsel, I will make it about what He says, not what I think
- I will listen and obey what He speaks to me
- It is better to leave complete honesty about my life in a safe arena with safe people
- It's not wrong to question those in authority as long as I do it with love, respect, and honor – and then walk away released from the matter
- It's not my place to police or judge what I view as err in another, but to pray, love and bless the God that is in them

- (and this is a hard one) I will keep my opinions to myself
- Trust is full of unimagined provision: I will do my best to live in it, God being my Helper!

To rest in confidence that He's begun a good work in us, we will be - must be - challenged in those things we think we know, what we speak, how we act and that to which what we give ourselves. No Truth becomes or remains ours, uncontested. I think if our earthly existence were only about the salvation of our soul, God would have taken us on to heaven the moment we confessed Him as Savior. Before He redeemed us, we knew mostly robbery of the portion God had initially designed for us. Life taught us to lie down, shut up and give in. God's Nature is always about redemption and of more than just our soul; He is also interested in the lost moments, gifts, ideas and contributions we were to have brought with us. We cannot believe that we each came into being because He needed one more person on the earth. No, we each brought something with us – something the world needed and He purposed to provide through our hands. Once the robbery happened, life after salvation became the vehicle of redemption for those lost parts of us.

Most could say we didn't know we needed a Savior until life taught us that we didn't have what it takes to live it on our own, and I'm not talking about personal resources. Even a rich man will come to know himself to be an emotional and spiritual pauper. Redemption changes us, must change us. If we cannot say that, then perhaps we are depending on our resources instead of the One who knows our needs. If, however, we have changed, acting and reacting a little more like Him, we can be confident that He will continue to perfect it through the process we call Redemption – never-ending Redemption.

Open and Release

"For men will be lovers of self…holding to a form of godliness, although they have denied its power…always learning and never able to come to the knowledge of the truth." (2 Timothy 3:2a, 5a, 7)

You have most likely been described as *religious* by someone in your family, friends or neighbors if you know God, have made Him a part of your everyday life, speak of Him, prayer or answers to prayer. There is, however, a big difference between being religious and being godly. Religion offers a finely crafted set of rules, doctrines, and interpretations. The purpose of doctrine lays in the hope its followers will agree on what was considered to be important issues. I don't have a problem with that; except that it very often becomes the problem between denominations and a common reason the world points its finger and says "Religious." Denominations don't agree, so they barely tolerate one another. That can be confusing to most within the church, let alone those on the outside of the church. Religions often make an issue out of the *what's* and *how's* at the expense of the **Who**.

The Pharisees and Sadducees of Jesus's day had become experts at making and keeping religious rules, yet Jesus called them a "brood of vipers." Their slavish attention to the rules and carefully attended righteousness had led most of them to live as judgmental and vindictive keepers of the Law, having reduced even that to a club by which they might maintain control. A set of rules or doctrines, no matter how finely written, can never save your soul and sanctify your life toward a purpose higher than what its limited interpretation might suggest. Learning about God and His ways is far from knowing God, that concept boiling down to a fair assessment of the difference between being religious and being godly.

We now live in an age where knowledge has become a concept highly revered, some even allowing it reasonable to conclude knowledge has replaced God, for He is dead. Professing themselves to be wise they have become fools (see Romans 1:22). Rattling words from vapid minds make philosophic conclusions that these lovers of *self* have become as a god, others serving a cause, ideal, or doctrine that will either take His place or lead one quickly to Him through death as a martyr. What a confusing world we live in where some make a religion out of denying God; while others kill each other in His Name, each claiming *right* is on their side. Many know about Him, hanging eternity on doctrines, rules and rote; hoping it is enough to follow the rules and be good. "I have seen all the works which have been done under the sun, and behold, all is vanity and striving after wind." (Ecclesiastes 1:14) Sometimes I wonder what God thinks about those things done, "in His Name." I would suppose, being God, He is not surprised that man has brought himself to such an impasse. He is, after all, "...the Alpha and the Omega, the first and the last, the beginning and the end." (Revelation 22:13)

Though the days seem filled with destruction, God remains in control; enabling the Remnant of salt and light to stay the hand of the destroyer through a personal relationship with the Son, the only door to salvation and eternity. "Jesus said to him, 'I am the way, and the truth, and the life; no one comes to the Father but through Me.'" (John 14:6)

And so, having said much, how might this be relevant to the godly man who stands in the shadow of evil with little in his hand? I think first, and foremost, we recognize that although there surely is a battle, it is not ours, but God's. Then, open our hand and release what is lays within, letting it flow generously and without restraint, praying that God will bless it with an increase. Not even the widow's mite was too small or insignificant in the hands of He to whom she gave it. We have overlooked the "...but God" if we consider any portion we have to give is too small. Only that which remains ungiven has no life in it. James says this, "Therefore to the one who knows the right thing to do and does not do it, to him it is sin." (James 4:17)

We cannot demand a change in the thoughts, affairs or actions of any man and expect compliance; all we have are seeds to plant. But, who can know the measured result in that which we freely give into His hand; nor is it important that we should. It's better that we simply give what we can out of a heart that expects nothing in return. The hand that casts a seed upon the winds of faith may never see the harvest. Neither does it need to do so. "Give and it will be given to you. They will pour into your lap a good measure - pressed down, shaken together, and running over. For by your standard of measure it will be measured to you in return." (Luke 6:38)

What Grandma Said

"And do not be conformed to this world, but be transformed by the renewing of your mind, so that you may prove what the will of God is, that which is good and acceptable and perfect." (Romans 12:2)

It's morning in Iowa – a beautiful day so far, even though the threat of humidity lay as a foggy blanket upon the still surface of our small lake this morning. It promises a muggy day, not my favorite, so I tended early to a few outside chores, readying myself for that hour when I will look for a shade tree under which to snap my beans and then lose my thoughts to a book.

It's quiet this morning, little beyond the sound of our resident Jenny Wren scolding the Catbird that slipped into the birdbath - which sits in her *territory* - for a quick splash. Our evenings of late have not been so quiet, although I must confess that little of nature's song is noise to me. Late summer is the season the Cicadas ply the evening with their song. This year their music sings a different tune to my ears for they have spoken a Truth my soul longs to ponder. Let me explain.

Each of us began our years in a family with its own set of habits, mindsets, perceptions and accepted truths. Whether it was the traditional mom and dad upbringing or another type of family, it does not matter. We are influenced, and thereby form our fundamental beliefs, by those who raised us. These made up the foundation from which we spring toward life. Questioning little, we forge the collection of, as yet, untried beliefs from which our soul makes our future choices. Some of these accepted conventions will serve us well; but some not so much for they were just wrong, wrong, wrong.

Let me give a small example: In the late summer, the quiet of evening gives way to what my family always called the Locust Song. It is their mating call; each male contracting/relaxing membranes in song, hoping to catch some female's attention. My grandmother - who knew and was right about everything - called them "Locusts," so I too called them Locusts. If anyone called them Cicadas, I secretly believed them to be wrong. I would not have challenged them because I knew the term to be correct in other parts of the country – but ours were Locusts because my Grandmother - and therefore the rest of us - called them Locusts. There was even an old saying that attended the arrival of our Locust Song; that being that we could expect six more weeks of summer before the first frost. It turns out that what my family called this evening songster was just as wrong as its weather prediction. They are not, never have been Locusts, but Cicadas; Locusts are a type of Grasshopper that swarms. My point for our consideration is that accepted family truth is very often wrong, and wisdom requires that what we believe had better be based on something more substantial than what Grandma said.

We are to present ourselves to God as the "...living and holy sacrifice..." (Romans 12:2) Paul talks about. The *self* we bring to lay before the Lord knows only the established and accepted habits of the world in which it grew. It had not served us particularly well, for most of what we had to lay upon the altar of Salvation was unrealized dreams, disappointment and a soul stripped of confidence. Even those who came with dollars to spare, success and its trappings do not feel otherwise. No matter how well kept our outside may look, few arrive intact from what life has dealt. Our soul demands to know where it belongs, a commodity that cannot be supplied from any source apart from Him. Whatever life has built or broken, bring Him that. It's all He asks!

May we never forget the change we came seeking in the first place. I brought a lot of "locusts" with me – if you catch my meaning. They were my beliefs, not necessarily because I'd made them by choice but because they were the accepted convention of family and/or society. Not all of them served me well. I learned to welcome that in Him I am being "...transformed by the renewing of your mind..." (Romans 12:2). Thankfully, He meant just that – transformed. Every preconceived idea, notion, ideology we hold will, little by little, be challenged and rooted out or, on more rare occasions, confirmed as Truth. Much as I loved her, I am not my Grandmother's study anymore; but a child of Promise, possessor of that "...measure of faith" (Romans 12:3) that transforms me.

Knowing this has given even more meaning to Joel's words, "Then I will make up to you for the years that the swarming locust has eaten...the creeping...stripping...gnawing locusts..." (Joel 2:25). He is restoring my soul, returning to me those things I had considered eternally lost because of the lies I had believed. This year the "Locust Song" has a different tune; a reminder of His faithful melody of the restoration of those truths that might have been lost to me forever - but were not!

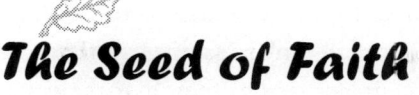

The Seed of Faith

"Therefore as you have received Christ Jesus the Lord, so walk in Him, having been firmly rooted and now being built up in Him and established in your faith, just as you were instructed, and overflowing with gratitude. See to it that no one takes you captive through philosophy and empty deception..." (Colossians 2:6 – 8a)

One might think that being long in experience would make the walk of faith easy – that perhaps somewhere along the way faith went on automatic pilot and just happened. It doesn't seem to work that way, faith needing to be refreshed and renewed for every occasion. I think as we grow in trust and experience we learn certain faith-principles that do come to our aid – if we remember to apply them, cease the urge to over-think or over-analyze, trying to anticipate every move. Faith will rarely make sense to our flesh or our common sense.

I've learned a lot about faith from my husband. One example: he flies a small ultralight airplane, and I'm afraid of heights; well, it's not so much the height as it is the unbidden and unexplainable anxiety of falling from them. And yet I have climbed into his plane, buckled myself in and enjoyed every moment of skimming high above the patchwork fields of green in the Iowa sunshine. Some thought to that regard helped me realize I trusted his knowledge and skill as a pilot more than the fear. That is a valuable and revealing lesson about faith to anyone who has felt the grip of fear. Whatever we put our trust in has the power. Each occasion we face in life holds to the same truth. Fear is the enemy of faith, robbing hope and peace in the process. Faith that consistently gives a place for fear to dwell has already decided its fate. It does not move forward, nor back, merely awaits what it already *knew* would happen. Job said, "For what I fear comes upon me, and what I dread befalls me." (Job 3:25) That is a sobering thought, that fear might have the power to provide a dwelling place to the very thing we say we don't want.

It was neither God's intent nor provision that faith would be a servant to fear; that's an evil plan that serves no one but the robber. Every seed carries within it the potential for unlimited abundance, but the return is contingent upon where one has planted it, or if they've planted it at all. God endowed each one of us with a seed of faith, a measure. It comes small, unformed and untried, like any seed, but the potential it carries locked within it is unlimited. One would have to agree, however, that the conditions into which we plant it, the attitudes of our mind and choices of our flesh in which we gave it room to grow, would affect its health and ability to come to maturity. The nature of the Christ that dwells with us is to plant! Plant abundantly, freely casting the seed He gave us into joy, trust, wisdom, good works, and always into a faith that trusts that He is the One that breathes life into His Promises.

It's an enigma to consider that a heart and mind so grateful to be redeemed could run so fast to give any part of it away. Paul wrote to the Colossians about giving their faith away to "philosophy and empty deception" (see Colossians 2:8). He did so with good reason. The Greek influence of the times had made a *religion* of philosophy, elevating the mind to a height and position that argued against faith in anything other than one's thoughts, concepts, and control. Fear always creates a void that demands to be filled. With what - remains the eternal question of humanity.

Paul had, by personal experience, answered that question because of an intimate encounter with Christ's forgiveness and faithfulness. He could write to the Colossians about the emotions of fear, guilt, and dread because he'd known them and knew deliverance from their threat and their grip. When he said "...that their hearts may be encouraged..." (Colossians 2:2) it was because he had known the need of encouragement. When he talked about being knit in love, the full assurance of understanding resulting in true knowledge; (see Colossians 2:2) he spoke out of a forgiven heart that has already walked that path ahead of them into "...God's mystery...that is, Christ Himself, in whom are hidden all the treasures of wisdom and knowledge." (Colossians 2:2b,3) He knew the faithful deliverance that accompanied every need.

We too have walked where Paul once walked, and we also will choose where, in what, whom – or Whom - we will plant our seeds of faith, our deep-down confidence. In the wisdom of man, the fear that what we want will never come to pass; or in "Gods mystery, that is Christ Himself in whom are hidden all the treasures of wisdom and knowledge." He knew our path and made us well-equipped to walk upon it – according to the "...stability of your faith in Christ. As you, therefore, have received Christ Jesus as Lord, so walk in Him, having been firmly rooted and now being built up in Him and established in your faith in Christ" (Colossians 2:5) Two paths lay in front of every man - let us wisely choose where to plant our foot.

Cracking Your Hedge

"Do not give what is holy to dogs and do not throw your pearls before swine, or they will trample them under their feet, and turn and tear you to pieces." (Matthew 7:6)

Most of us as children probably met with some form of bullying. Kids can be quite adept at it, adults too; not all of it the kind that leaves bruises on your shins. It is the bruises on the heart and soul that leave the most lasting scars.

I grew up in a small farming community so rode the bus to the Community School that sat in the middle of one church, one grocery store and the handful of houses that made up our tiny town. Even calling it a town is a stretch of courtesy. 14 kids made up my class of nine boys and five girls. We did not think about being close; it was just that we were all we had so we never really considered it. At the beginning of 5th grade, we got a new student, Nancy; whose dresses were more stylish than ours, they were cuter, and she was too. The boys loved her. To the girls she was bossy and controlling, changing the whole dynamics of our little class. It was Nancy who now decided who was *in* and who was *out*. For the first time in our lives, a bully led and, unless one dared to defy her, one did as she commanded. Nobody defied her, first of all, because we had no experience to call upon and second, the fear of being isolated from our little group. It was just easier to take your turn of being *out* and hope for a better tomorrow.

Is a bully born or created? Created, I think; most likely as a way to maintain a sense of control or escape the pain, emotional deserts or judgments of the lives so many of our young endure, but over which they have no control. Once a bully-in-the-making tastes the power of another's fear and sense submission, it's as addicting as any drug.

As Christian brothers and sisters, judging one another could rightly be considered spiritual bullying. It's not the plan God intends for our spiritual family, although He does have a lot to say about it. Redemption levels the ground at the Cross. Because we all stand cleansed in the same degree, judging has no platform on which to stand. It happens though, this spiritual bullying. Might it spring from a similar need for the recognition and control hungered for by the school-yard bullies of childhood? That it springs from the depths of an evil well cannot be disputed or misunderstood. If God is in control, - and He is - He doesn't need our help to point out the faults of another. He calls us to be like Him, to share the Gospel of salvation through Jesus Christ, to give service to the church and those in need. Beyond that, it might be considered prudent to keep our attention on the log in our own eye (see Matthew 7:4). Jesus didn't mince words, saying, "You hypocrite, first take the log out of your own eye, and then you will see clearly enough to take the speck out of your brother's eye." (Matthew 7:5)

The next verse requires some thought, for it cannot be considered apart from the words that directly precede it nor those that follow. How then might judging be tied to, "Do not give what is holy to dogs, and do not throw your pearls before swine..."? (Matthew 7:6a)

A spiritual bully does not care about the speck in another's eye, beyond the fact that he feels it reduces the weighty significance of the log in his own. Does he feel released once he's made the shift of attention to another? Does he feel relieved of his own pressing need for restoration because of what he's judged as *worse*? No one stands outside the need for redemption, but the quicksand world of a *judger*, puts him in peril of missing his portion of it because he trained himself to avoid his own need for it. Judging cracks our spiritual hedge of protection, leaving that treasured part of ourselves - the pearls - vulnerable to dogs and swine.

Many years have passed since the end of 6th grade when Nancy moved. I never saw her again; but, never did those of us who had endured her presence become the same innocents we had been before she came. I would not count her among my friends, but she was a good mentor of sorts. I don't often think of Nancy anymore. If she does come to mind, I bless and thank her. She taught me some great lessons: the difference between a mean spirit and a gentle one, the effect of judging versus the weight of acceptance. In every hand a staff is held; one rises to make way for war, the other to peace. Choose wisely!

Are We There Yet?

"…Keep sound wisdom and discretion, so that they will be life to your soul… Then you will walk in your way securely and your foot will not stumble." (Proverbs 3:21b, 23)

Although one may have walked with the Lord for many years, I doubt if anyone would say they felt any sense of having *arrived*. If we've been paying attention, we should have honed some skills, become wiser in our response to the voices that sometimes threaten our security and our peace. We learn to answer them quicker and with more confidence – if we've been paying attention. Change should be the constant companion of growth. It often seems a slow process, but one designed to consistently mature us in the confidence and wisdom of the One who will never leave us or forsake us. We call Him Holy Spirit, Comforter, Advocate, Counsellor, Teacher, and Friend; but only because we've needed Him to be those things to us - and He has been all of them at various times. One who learns to search for Him knows He is not difficult to find, our reminder close at hand when we feel alone or without resources. He is there in times of trouble and times of rejoicing as well.

Because of His great love for us, He will not leave us subject to the source of our downfalls without gently pointing out the need for change – nor the not-so-gentle when we will not listen. No amount of experience in the Lord will lessen our need to keep growing. We have much to learn, and sometimes we end up being our biggest hindrance to the peace and security we say we so diligently seek. It works best when we relax and little and look for joy in the ride.

It's not always so easy to do in a world where quiet and order is often fleeting. It's not just concerns of a personal nature that trouble our heart, very often we are drawn away from our center of peace by the heart-wrenching needs of family, friends, or church. There is enough trouble to go around, but I have found that if we gaze at needs long enough, they will consume us. Our thoughts and opinions soon become thin and brittle unless planted in His care. Why we would repeatedly give ourselves to the problem I do not know, would it not be better to give ourselves to the place where Hope dwells?

"Elijah came near to all the people and said, 'How long will you hesitate between two opinions? If the Lord is God, follow Him; but if Baal, follow him.' But the people did not answer him a word." (1 Kings 18:21) It was not a good season for the people of the land, those who served the Lord God and the evil-doer alike. The drought was severe, the leadership of the country was questionable and the people – well, the people were ready to jump one way or the other according to the prevailing wind of the day, so did not answer Elijah a word. They found their beliefs trapped between following God or King Ahab and his 450 prophets of Baal plus the 400 prophets of the Asherah, who ate at Jezebel's table. The people just sat on the proverbial fence, waiting to see which way the wind was going to blow before they committed themselves. In actuality, what they settled for revealed more about them than about the situation they found themselves living in. A refusal to commit had committed them already. At the very least they had given themselves to compromise, at most to idolatry. Either would require their uttermost farthing before it would spit them out broken and alone.

Now when I was young, we had an outhouse. The path to it soon became so familiar that I could walk it without thinking, blindfolded if need be. But no matter how familiar the way, it still led to the outhouse. Perhaps wisdom would make the destination a priority before she chose the path on which to walk.

The enemies of God made the way seem familiar, smooth and comfortable. It seemed to take a long time before the people realized their refusal to choose had chosen already. They fooled no one but themselves if they thought God wouldn't hold them to account. "A fool does not delight in understanding, but only in revealing his own mind. When a wicked man comes, contempt also comes, and with dishonor comes scorn. The words of a man's mouth are deep waters; the fountain of wisdom is a bubbling brook." (Proverbs 18:2-4) The words we say, the choices we make today lay the path we will walk upon tomorrow.

The Lord God is constant in his faithfulness to us, but He can only transform those portions we give Him, and that requires us to be honest with ourselves and with Him. He already knows our heart and mind, what have we got to gain by refusing? Every experience we place in His hand, whether we consider it to be a loss or a gain, works the righteousness of God within us.

The Measure of Happiness

"If you know these things, you are blessed if you do them." (John 13:17)

By the time Jesus spoke these words; His days upon the earth were growing to a close. It was the Feast of the Passover as Jesus gathered His disciples for what we call The Last Supper. Peter was undone, feeling unworthy; I'm sure, as Jesus knelt before him with a basin and towel to wash his feet. I'm not so sure I wouldn't be like Peter, laboring to lay down my unworthiness to such an intimate care. To a heart so aware of its lack, too much in touch with its failings, it seems to expose our wretched humanness that He would kneel before us. Jesus answered Peter, "...If I do not wash you, you have no part with Me." (John 13:8b)

We, humans, are a rowdy lot, scrambling our way through the merry-go-round of life, seeking to feel significant about who we are, what we have, what we do, or what makes us happy. Unless I'm missing the point, I think that whether the circumstances of life line up to make us happy is not the purpose of life anyway. Happiness is a wonderful feeling, but it comes, and it goes. We are far too inclined to measure the quality of our life, even the purpose of it, by whether it makes us *feel* happy. The chase to find happiness usually causes its seekers to miss so much along the way they more often than not end up frustrated and disappointed, thinking they must surely have missed something along and way – and that must be somebody's fault. I think it's when we begin to view the *pursuit of happiness* as a *right to be happy* that we get into trouble. Then it turns, becoming a devil that demands its right to be first, to sit upon the throne; insatiable, without regard to what the cost might be to family, duty, responsibility or wisdom. A trip down *Happiness Lane* will eventually cause us to lose sight of everything that would give our life value or meaning beyond the moment.

I looked up the word "happiness" in my Bible concordance and found it rarely mentioned, and then only as it relates to giving selflessly into the lives of others. It appears it is an emotion more suited to giving away than getting or having. As long as one measures happiness according to what they have or how life suits them from moment to moment, it remains fleeting. Feelings are not a good barometer for they do not measure value, or depth, or longevity - they are concerned only with keeping the self well fed, appeased and quiet.

As diverse as we appear on the surface, within the heart and soul of every one of us lay the same core of desires: we want to feel loved, safe and significant. We call it being happy. Jesus showed His disciples the key to that was to wash one another's feet (see John 13:14). When life is focused solely on who we are, what we have or need, there will never be quite enough; but a cup poured out upon the feet of another somehow returns to us in a measure, pressed down and running over. "If you know these things, you are blessed if you do them." (John 13:17)

If there is a secret to happiness, it is found buried in God and giving yourself - especially your self - to others. When we center our life in Him, rather than the issues of our own existence, He will establish both heart and soul in peace and joy; a more substantial and lasting reality than what we refer to as happiness. Only when we honestly trust the process of planting our life in God - regardless of the need to measure everything by how it makes us feel - can we truly enjoy those fleeting moments we call happiness. We are no longer a slave, dependent on the demands of feelings. Only then are we are at liberty to live with a sense of complete fulfillment and eternal purpose. "If you know these things, you are blessed if you do them." (John 13:17)

When Jesus washed the feet of the disciples, it was about a whole lot more than dirty feet. By doing so, He identified with each one and the journey that had brought them to that moment when He lifted each weary foot, refreshed it with life-giving water and carefully wiped it clean. Those intimate moments reflected the ministry and purpose of Christ to the world, each experience they had shared. It also served as a subtle anointing, preparation for what was to come; those moments when the Truth He was about to purchase on the Cross would be sent forth into the world upon the very feet He now washed. Born a man, lived as a man but always God, He never for a moment lost sight of Who He was, why He came or what it would mean. "...Do you know what I have done to you?" (John 13:12b) This is perhaps one of the most important questions any of us will answer.

Give them a King

"The Lord said to Samuel, 'Listen to the voice of the people in regard to all that they say to you, for they have not rejected you, but they have rejected Me from being king over them.'" (1 Samuel 8:7)

God's *chosen* were a people He knew and called His own, people who journeyed to and fought for the land He had promised them; one that was to be their own for all time. God's first choice for a system of government was that each family would govern their affairs. Families eventually became tribes with time, the leaders all descending back to a common male patriarch. It was not uncommon for three to four generations to live in the same household. Collectively their form of government was considered a Theocracy - meaning God led - the head of each family - elders - hearing for and making decisions for his entire household; the elders of various households joining together in making decisions that affected the whole of them, things like war and famine. These occasional needs to band together in one unit were put under the leadership of one person, referred to as Judge. This system, although not without its challenges, actually worked quite well for several thousand years, from Abraham to the days of Samuel, the Prophet.

Somewhere around 1000 B.C. the demands of the people brought about change. It says in 1 Samuel, "Now Samuel judged Israel all the days of his life." (1 Samuel 7:15) The following verses in chapter

8 tell that in his declining years he appointed his sons as judges, "His sons, however, did not walk in his ways, but turned aside after dishonest gain and took bribes and perverted justice." (I Samuel 8:3) That they were being be led by ungodly men ended with this demand from the elders of Israel. "...Behold you have grown old, and your sons do not walk in your ways. Now, appoint a king for us like all the nations." (I Samuel 8:5b) Displeased by their demands, Samuel prayed to the Lord, and He answered thus, "...Listen to the voice of the people...for they have not rejected you, but they have rejected Me from being king over them." (I Samuel 8:5)

No change comes unaccompanied; there is always a risk, a cost, and a reward. Wisdom counts the cost and balances the risk against the hoped-for reward. Making life-changing decisions is difficult enough when making them for our personal lives; impossible, I think when a man seeks to alter God's plan. But, the people had demanded a king. 1 Samuel 8:10-22 (paraphrased) says: God said, give them a king but tell them the cost: (1) He will reign over you; (2) take your sons for the military, (3) your daughters as servants. (4) He will do with you as he pleases; (5) take what property he desires, (6) a tenth of your income as taxes. The Lord concluded, (7) "Then you will cry out...but the Lord will not answer you in that day." (1 Samuel 8:18)

From the foundation of the world, God's Plan was for Redemption. Through one people, one Man, the whole of Mankind would know eternity: the Man, Christ Jesus. Neither time nor circumstances had altered God's Plan: but free will had chosen a road much harder to walk.

The choices of man are fickle and find humanity, these centuries later, with nothing changed: nations forge ahead, ever losing sight of God as governments continue imposing their will on the people in the manner their limited wisdom would dictate – the cost of it still borne by the people and future generations. By all appearances, we live in the wilderness of unending decline with only two gates out, one narrow, one wide. Both lead to eternity: salvation through Jesus Christ or the pit of destruction. Free will chooses the portal through which every man/woman will pass.

Not willing that any man should perish, (see 2 Peter 3:9) it is never too late to turn to God, to repent and call upon His Name; but nations do not repent. It is people who humble themselves, pray, seek His face and turn from their wicked ways (see 2 Chronicles 7:14) Then He will hear – God's ear is always bent low to hear the cry of repentance. The heart of man, his life, his nation and his world swings on the gate of repentance, revival our only hope in a world gone mad with hate, prejudice, violence, and war. Most of us wring our hands, not knowing what we could do about it. But, this I know to be true: if any man presents himself to God with the question that stirs in his heart, He will answer. Revival is a consuming fire, calling to the heart of men, one by one, for repentance. Only then can that man reach out his hand to restore peace. "He has told you, O man, what is good; and what does the Lord require of you, but to do justice, to love kindness, and to walk humbly with your God?" (Micah 6:8)

Repentance means: to turn from and go in another direction. And, though it may seem a small a thing in the face of the world's great need, the power that resides within the one by one that God calls, is always enough when it rests in His hand.

My Sneaky Flesh

"Therefore, if anyone is in Christ, he is a new creature; the old things passed away, behold new things have come." (2 Corinthians 5:17)

We raised one beautiful daughter. As with most young parents, we had no experience so bumbled along as best we could, making uncertain choices according to limited information. Those days there was no Ask-a-Nurse and no Google. Having found Christ as our Savior when she was about 6, our lives changed – a lot! We loved the church, the pastor, and the people; and soon our lives were centered on home and church.

Over the next few years, although I was unaware at the time, a subtle change began taking place in me. Whether from real or self-imposed expectations, I cannot say with clarity; but I began to feel a strong sense of responsibility that our family - and thereby our daughter - must portray Christ in the best possible light. That I was young and learning seems a poor excuse for the drive to live as examples of perfection. I was unaware that it was not only foolish but impossible, so feebly gave myself to the task. I used the only resource I knew to accomplish it – control. I was subtle, yes, but I was controlling, none the less. What an ugly picture that paints of me all written out here in black and white. Even after these many years that have since passed, were it not for Christ's forgiveness, I would be ashamed of myself. The Scripture says in Christ old things are passed away, but that is not an automatic with those firmly entrenched patterns and habits of the flesh, you know. A life lived by wiles and fulfilling the desires of our flesh doesn't automatically submit to the Christ within. If our life remains unenlightened, our habits and actions unchallenged, these patterns not only stay with us, they perfect their crafty skills and their argument to stay. I don't know why we would try to *Christianize* these old go-to habits; they carry the stink of death with them and have neither place nor purpose in the Redeemed.

I don't think that young mom was different than most who want the best for their children, but the line is fine between guidance and control. Guidance is about the child, helping them find the best possible path, to have the courage and permission to walk it. Control remains connected to the one who exerts it, its foremost concern not the other person but how they reflect upon you. It's an ugly and selfish truth.

If it were not for the Grace of God, I'm not sure any one of us could stand some of our past choices or actions. I got too caught up in how we looked to other people. I was the pastor's secretary, my husband on the Church Board; if we weren't perfect, what would people think? What awful pressures the flesh and unexamined soul will put upon us – and how very far away from God's plan for complete transformation and redemption they try to lead us.

When we are honest and sincere in our desire to know God, He does not withhold the truth from us or about us, especially in those areas where our flesh has become a hindrance to the very things we desire and say we seek. Control is fear all dressed up in its Sunday best; it argues that it *only wants what's best*. There is no justification for it, neither is there a bit of faith in the whole of it.

Since the real desire of my heart was to know God and walk in His revelation and Truth, He was faithful to me. When I saw control for what it was, for some days, I reeled beneath the weight and ugliness of what I had given myself to and what I had done to my child. I first asked God for forgiveness and then went to my 12-year-old daughter, confessed my sin and requested she forgive me. She answered me, "That's okay, Mom; you didn't know what you were doing." Oh my, what great wisdom the innocent spoke. She was right; I didn't know what I was doing. I gave up control that day and have since learned to keep a closer watch on my sneaky flesh. Old things may have passed away, but sometimes they still try to call to us from the grave.

I did find that faith is more certain in its outcome when we are honest with and about ourselves while seeking the things of God. Our daughter grew to be a wise and godly woman, one in whom dwells love, grace, and the vitality of God. Regardless of our inexperience, mistakes, and uncertainties, she survived us and overcame them all. Thanks to God's Grace and a child with a forgiving nature!

Greater Works

"I will give you the keys of the kingdom of heaven; and whatever you shall bind on earth shall have been bound in heaven, and whatever you shall loose on earth shall have been loosed in heaven." (Matthew 16:19)

I'm trying to put myself in Peter's place as I think about the scope of the ministry Jesus was preparing to leave in the hands of these few Apostles. How could it be that they, who knew little beyond their daily lives, whose spiritual understanding had been limited to the Law and the blood of sheep and goats, would change the world? I think it impossible for them in that day, or we in ours, if not for the revelation of the Holy Spirit which causes us to know and understand what we cannot conceive by our wisdom and understanding, nor do by our own hands.

Jesus always knew who He was and the purpose He came to establish. He knew the Cross, the door it would eternally open and the hands that would eventually hold the keys to the Kingdom. These men and those of us who would walk the path He christened with His Blood, would represent Him on earth where the forces of evil held reign. To a bit of salt, a little light – and the keys to the kingdom – the baton of authority passed. "Truly, truly, I say to you, he who believes in Me, the works that I do, he will do also; and

greater works than these he will do; because I go to the Father."
(John 14:12)

No one can act on behalf of another without: (1) a clear sense of
who they represent (2) confidence they speak for the authority that
stands behind them. These are issues we must settle in our heart
and mind before considering taking on spiritual battles. If not done
in the Name and authority of Jesus Christ, we shouldn't do it at
all. Flesh and blood cannot reveal these things, only the Father in
Heaven (see Matthew 16:17).

Peter understood Jesus was Messiah; he did not yet understand
what that would mean in the days going forward, the days when he
would fully comprehend the meaning of the name bestowed upon
him. Peter - or Petra – translates to, "small rock." It was never Peter
who was the foundation of the church; he was just the token pebble
of the church to come, all of us who would call Him, "... the Christ,
the Son of the living God." He is the foundation of the church. If
He entrusted the keys of the kingdom of heaven - the authority to
represent - into first Peter's hands and now our hands, what is it that
we are to do with them?

It is no stretch to understand the forces of evil that influence, agitate
and control our world. The news affirms them day by day. Jesus
said in John, "The thief comes only to steal and kill and destroy; I
came that they may have life, and have it abundantly." (John 10:10) I
think that means that although evil may walk the perimeter of our
life, don't rush out to meet it, keep our focus on that which gives
Life. My pastor's wife used to say, "Glance at evil but stare at God."
Learn to live with an attitude that affirms Christ as head of all and
the mediator between God and man (see I Timothy 2:5). We don't
have to fear any circumstance if we are confident in Who He is and
who we are in Him. The authority rests with Him, not us. It may
be our hands that touch, our mouth that speaks, but it is always the

Christ that works through us. Time and practice will confirm the truth of His authority in us.

We battle a wily foe, one whose favorite weapon is to divide and confuse as a base from which to conquer: (1) Divide us from other like-minded believers, (2) Divide us from our sense of spiritual authority in Christ; (3) Confuse the purpose and use of it.

"For our struggle is not against flesh and blood, but against the rulers, against the powers, against the world forces of this darkness, against the spiritual forces of wickedness in the heavenly places." (Ephesians 6:12) Humans may be the feet that run to do evil, but they are not the enemy against whom we should stand. Let us keep our prayers to bind and loose where they belong, against principalities and powers and unseen forces in high places. The battle is always in the realm of the spiritual, and if we allow feelings, fear, hurt or judgment to rule our prayers, it is akin to watering them down to tinkling brass and sounding cymbals.

We are not able to live in a manner that avoids spiritual battles. We don't have to go looking for them, they will find us. When they come, we'd best know the One we represent, what Christ did and in whose hand He gave the keys of the kingdom of heaven. Be not afraid for He has equipped us well to stand for every occasion.

Let There Be Peace

"Do not think that I came to bring peace on earth; I did not come to bring peace but a sword. (Matthew 10:34)

It's late in the evening, December 24th and you've wrapped your last package, placed it lovingly beneath a green tree bulging with the ornaments, garland, tinsel, and lights you had so recently gathered your family to put there. Well, all the family but Jean, for she'd opted to spend the evening with her boyfriend. You sigh; you'd so looked forward to that evening of togetherness you'd written in your imagination: cocoa with little marshmallows, some Christmas carols, laughter, warmth, and peace. The boys hadn't ended up wrestling on the floor in your imagined evening. The angel, the object of their dispute, hadn't lost her halo, nor had your husband *had enough*. You stare at the lone card sitting on the mantle of the unlit fire you had so hopefully laid and read the words "Peace on Earth" once more and wonder; what peace and in whose world?

It is easy enough to grow weary of the controversy that always seems to swirl too close to the life we had built in our hopes. The hopes where the family gets along, no one is sick or dying, money wasn't tight or non-existent, no shots rang out, and no flag-draped casket reminded us of war. War and peace: opposing concepts forever linked in the affairs of Mankind.

In Matthew, Jesus spoke these words to His disciples, "Behold, I send you out as sheep in the midst of wolves, so be shrewd as serpents and innocent as doves." (Matthew 10:16) Is He telling us to keep our wary wits about the choices we make, the people to whom we listen and the things unto which we give our heart? Does He counsel us that in the midst of the swirling helter-skelter, we are to keep ourselves at peace and do no harm? That our heart must both expect and prepare for the war that follows throughout the whole of His passage here? "I did not come to bring peace, but a sword," (Matthew 16:34) and those words are very often borne out in families. There will be times in life where we will be challenged to forego the very thing we tried to preserve – family - and for His sake. Having had the opportunity to experience familial division, let me interject that it leaves one feeling confused and unable to adequately explain how such a seemingly small happening could have caused such a big war.

As a girl growing up, I dared not bring a complaint to my mom about something someone had said about me without hearing the words, "Sticks and stones may break your bones, but words will never hurt you." I think she could have added, "...unless you choose to let them." Her advice seems to be wisdom from which our current generation appears to have separated themselves. Plainly said, we've become thin-skinned. Puffed up on our own opinions and concepts – sometimes even about the things of God - it is easy enough to lose sight of peace when *right* becomes the issue. As others begin to weigh in with their opinions, the often repeated tale of offense grows to unrecognizable proportions and opposing factions' war; not with weapons made of steel, but words, emotions, and seeds of hurt left unredeemed in the hearts of each. It's a slippery slope!

There is little peace in this world so steeped in controversy. Perhaps that's why Jesus spoke so much about it – there is so little to be had.

Into that world, we are called to "...take up his cross and follow Him." (Matthew 16:24b) What then does your cross look like – and how does my cross appear? What suffering, hurts or offenses have been nailed there, and by whose hand? Forgiveness rests in the Cross that bears upon it the stains of His redeeming Blood. Surely it must be easier to lay it all upon that Cross than continue to bear the burden of heaviness that weight down a heart who will not forgive. "He who has found – *keeps* - his life will lose it, and he who has lost - *gives away* - his life for My sake will find it." (see Matthew 10:39).

If we must choose – and we must – let us choose carefully. And, if we are to forego peace for a season, let it be because we seek a greater purpose. Sometimes it takes a little time before everyone is willing to lay down the weapons of the war they view as *an offense*. Give a sacrifice of time, without expectation. "And whoever...gives to one of these little ones even a cup of cold water to drink, truly I say to you, he shall not lose his reward." (Matthew 10:42) Yes, let there be peace on earth!

On Time and Fully Complete

"I would have despaired unless I had believed that I would see the goodness of the Lord in the land of the living. Wait for the Lord; be strong and let your heart take courage; yes, wait for the Lord." (Psalm 27:13, 14)

Most of our lives revolve around waiting. Our mom was probably the first one that taught us the meaning of the word as we pulled upon her shirt tail to make our demand on her busy morning. At school, we waited, at the water fountain, in the lunch line, for recess. We grew, we waited: for a chance to play on the team, for a good college, that special someone, a job, recognition, a home of our own. We do a lot of waiting; you'd think we'd get used to it, learn to do it gracefully.

I wonder what David thought as he waited with his father's sheep on the hillside, as he knelt before Samuel awaiting the oil with which he was anointed. He waited before Goliath with stones and sling in the ready, in the cave at Engedi, when he cut off the edge of Saul's robe (see 1 Samuel). What did David think about when waiting on the rooftop as Bathsheba bathed, or when he waited for word of Uriah? David did a lot of waiting; but the most important moments, those that changed his life forever, were those he spent waiting upon the Lord. Perhaps this is the final proving ground of a life well-schooled in waiting; what we waited on will bear out that we waited for.

Some of us are better at waiting than others. Even though we've lost the choice of *when* in the waiting, the *how* becomes a telling exposure of our spiritual dynamics. Some do it gracefully, considering there is much to gain in the time taken to get them from where they are to where they believe the Promise means to deliver them. Some stomp their feet, flail their arms and set themselves to whining how nothing ever works out for them and it's just not fair. The waiting process will be very different for each of them, so will what each of them takes with them going forward in life.

A favorite Scripture of many is "Delight yourself in the Lord; and He will give you the desires of your heart." (Psalm 37:4)) It's not unusual that we focus more on the "desires" part than on the "delight" but that one is effectively tied to the other David had learned by personal experience. We will learn it as well. His life was not without great challenge, nor was it devoid of death, despair, intrigue and the agony that sometimes gripped his soul as he wrestled back and forth between "My God, my God, why have You forsaken me?..." (Psalm 22:1) and "The Lord is my shepherd, I shall not want." (Psalm 23:1) Somewhere in the waiting, the seeds planted in the *delighting* times began to take root and grow in Him.

Somewhere along our line of waiting, we must begin to face the truth about our self, the stumbling blocks, our attitudes, lack or the sin we may be allowing to color our path. The only hope of deliverance lays in being honest; with ourselves first and then Him. It's a choice we make: will we ask for His help to overcome the hindrances that seem to dog our steps or keep repeatedly stumbling around the same old *bush* on our own? It's vital that we assess what we are contributing to - or robbing from - the make-up of this faith-life we hope to build; the one that will allow us to delight ourselves in the Lord. If we say we want the things of God but chase after evil in the hidden parts of our flesh, in our attitudes and thought life, they will trip us up somewhere, sometime, somehow. Desires rarely just spring forth, but rest on the foundation built to receive them.

David's flesh made huge mistakes, his soul despaired and his hands hung down – and yet his feet learned to dance before the Lord, his God. He sought deliverance, confessed his lack and took his lumps; but if we were to look up the lineage of Jesus Christ, there stands David among them.

We are never defined by the worst of us, rather to whose account we have laid the charge. Christ forgives, He redeems, and He restores. To everyone who can "delight themselves in Him" the times of waiting had been but a fleeting moment that awaited the desires He fulfilled within us – on time and fully complete.

Out of the Heart

"Finally, brethren, whatever is true...honorable...right...pure... lovely...of good repute...if there is any excellence and if anything worthy of praise, dwell on these things." (Philippians 4: 8)

I'm not exactly sure of all of the *whys* of it, but I do not readily talk about some of the things that make up my past, those days before I knew the need for a Savior. It's not that I'm ashamed. I know that some of my worst mistakes have made the most significant contribution to the days that lay beyond them. I would not change them if I could. I also know that neither my character nor my future was decided or defined by the worst of my failures. They have built me into the person I am, and I could not expect to be the same if I were to lose any one of my former experiences. I can keep these things in perspective, knowing that no matter how vital or how devastating any one event, even one season of life may have seemed, it did not have the power to predict or define the whole – nor did it last forever. We are the products of many experiences, and our future is predicted more by where, or in Whom, we choose to lay our past.

Perhaps some things about me belong only to God and me; things that molded me and contributed significantly to who I am as a person, the way I think, act and react. Those things built character in me and resiliency. "As far as the east is from the west, so far has

He removed our transgressions from us." (Psalm 103:12) Once He removes the stain of sin from our past, those experiences become nothing more than building material in the hands of the Master Carpenter, becoming the framework upon which He builds a new creation. I do not expose that casually or without good cause for its value is too great, and few would understand why. Not everything needs to become fodder for the lips of idle busybodies who would not purpose to speak of the trials of my life that God might be glorified. Gossip somehow seems to lessen the value of what He has done. Let us be prudent when exposing our greatest challenges and biggest victories. If the Lord opens the door to share, do so with abandon, because He wants to use our testimony. Otherwise, hold your peace. "When there are many words, transgression is unavoidable, but he who restrains his lips is wise." (Proverbs 10:19)

It is wisdom to live with an attitude of transparency, nothing hidden; but there is a fine line between being transparent and being foolish. We often tell too much and most of it without good cause. At times we rattle on about intimate thoughts and feelings, small hurts and imagined slights just for the momentary sense of emotional release it gives us; serving no purpose other than burdening another or giving the enemy of our soul ammunition for a further accusation. Usually, our conversation proves an accurate reflection of where our mind has been allowed to dwell.

The past will always counsel our future; not all of it reflecting the level of Redemption to which we might have aspired. Old habits sometimes die hard. We will all have memories that, on occasion, spring out of our heart and strike us dumb; for we had considered it dead and gone. How is it that those things we had thought to be dead could speak with such vicious abandon? Though my day is still young, I have already faced the choice to reel my tongue back from the brink of a less than gracious observation. I did so and no doubt altered the path my day might have taken. It's a sneaky foe that steals our moments and changes our path; thoughts casually offered, settling into a groove like a broken record, the only way to stop it is to lift up the needle. The mind can be a dangerous place to dwell for it seems to have feet of its own. The flesh and the devil are sneaky foes, dragging us to places our heart never intended to go. "Watch over your heart with all diligence, for from it flow the springs of life." (Proverbs 4:23)

Paul speaks to the heart, what has gone into it and what comes out, when he says, "And the peace of God, which surpasses all comprehension, will guard your hearts and your minds in Christ Jesus. Finally, brethren, whatever is true...honorable...right... lovely...of good repute... excellence...worthy of praise, dwell on these things." (Philippians 4:7, 8) I confess to finding this level of noble conduct a challenge which I struggle to maintain in the day-to-day. That which flows out of my heart and across my tongue will lay the path upon which my feet will walk today. Let wisdom be the order of the day.

More than Sufficient

"You shall consecrate yourselves therefore and be holy, for I am the Lord your God. You shall keep My statutes and practice them; I am the Lord who sanctifies you." (Leviticus 20:7, 8)

The young woman across the table from me had shared some of her heart, to which I had made just a few observations. It undid me when she placed her hand on mine and said, "Oh, you are so wise."

I almost fell in my coffee. Me? Wise? I know too well how often I've failed and that I've learned a thing or two along the way, but to hear someone call such hard-won experience "wisdom" was more than a little unsettling. When, in my walk with the Lord, had my quest for enough knowledge and experience to put my own life together and set my personal lack to flight, become Bread for another whose soul was hungry?

I consider myself blessed to have accepted Christ under the care and ministry of people who diligently sought the Lord, read and believed His Word and expected that any new member of the family of God would just naturally do the same. Much of what they accepted as a standard for the life of one who walked in the ways of Christ is seldom taught and rarely spoken in most churches at this more contemporary season. I don't hear much about "claiming the Promises"; those Scriptures of promise found in God's Word for change, provision and blessing for our life, family, and future; the ones by which we were once encouraged to write our name. The spiritual power and protection found through "pleading the Blood" is a term I no longer hear. My faith rests upon it; it is the foundation that affirms the authority and victory that Christ won on the Cross when His shed Blood satisfied heaven and earth. To *plead* the Blood simply means to *answer the charge*; whether my past, my sin or the devil made the accusation. And yet, the Blood is rarely mentioned, *pleading* it even less so. It seems a rare occasion for parishioners to leave the church with a good dose of conviction over our sin and to deny ourselves anything often appears to have become a foreign concept. Growth and progress must always attend any walk forward; but how often is progress made at the expense of specific foundational blocks upon which our soul might safely rest?

To come to the turning point where we accept the reality that we need a Savior is one of life's most profound and essential moments, but to somehow consider salvation to be an end would be akin to receiving but then ignoring the wealth of a great inheritance. Salvation is not an end; rather, the beginning of His process to sanctify our soul. Sanctification is a term not often heard in the church anymore. If mentioned at all, it is more likely to be referred to "the process" of becoming like Christ. And, if it's the same thing, I have no issue with what it's called.

Webster says sanctification means: to set apart as holy.

Perhaps an over-simplification of the meaning is: to be used for the purpose for which it was first designed. That would be to worship our God, have fellowship with Him, know His Word and live according to its edicts and Promise, do unto others, serve God and man and live life to the fullest potential He had designed for you. Easy enough to write about transformation, hard enough to cooperate with it when the old man of flesh - this demanding and selfish flesh I might add - battles and seeks to undermine every resolve.

The call of the Redeemed is to be like Him. Those first feelings of joy and hope will soon face a challenge when the habits we had spent long years perfecting raise their head and present their case, hoping to remain in charge. We may want to change, know we need to change; but the old ways do not gracefully consent to the new. Compromise is usually one of the first and most lasting temptations our new-found life in Christ will face. It's a lie to believe an old enemy can dwell in our new *land* and not influence or affect our actions and choices. Paraphrased, Hebrews 11:15 says that if the saints of old had been thinking of (dwelling on) the country (former life) they had come from, they might have had the opportunity to have returned. I find that a scary and intimidating proposition for the real truth of the land I came from is that it held me hostage to fear, control, hopelessness, anger, and strife. It contains nothing of value which I would embrace if I had the opportunity to return. I like living in a land that has a future, an inheritance, and a promise. I've never considered that giving my life to eternity caused me to lose anything of worth. I prefer to remember that within His confines I've discovered the liberty to walk the path I was always designed to tread and to enjoy my assigned portion. His provision has ever proved to be more than sufficient.

Unerring Order

"For we know in part and we prophecy in part...When I was a child, I used to speak like a child, think like a child, reason like a child; when I became a man, I did away with childish things. For now we see in a mirror dimly, but then face to face; now I know in part, but then I shall know fully just as I also have been fully known." (1 Corinthians 13:9, 11, 12)

Arising at first light this morning, although taken with the beauty the world held as that first thin thread of light washed the horizon, I was not shocked at its coming. The birds sang, the breeze played lightly among the summer leaves and in the distance, a rooster crowed his delight at the rising sun. That the world has design and order is an expected part of my day.

Genesis does not constrain itself to the process nor elaborate on details, but merely states that God created. It does not say there were materials at hand, so my thought on that matter has always been that the substance of Creation came from the only Source of material He had at hand – Himself. But that's just my thought and based on nothing more than the desire of a finite mind to explain how something can come from nothing. It cannot! I am often perplexed that science seemingly avoids that conundrum when its point of origin skips Creation and asks its subscribers to begin at a black hole, a big bang or an amoeba that somehow accidentally created itself. What an amazing coincidence that that which is perfectly aligned in composition, design, and order that is without error managed to substantiate its perfection out of such a tenuous and uncertain beginning.

There's not a thing about Creation that is haphazard. All we know of life and substance has order and affirms a distinction that it is Divine in both purpose and precision. Everything, from the DNA of man, plants, and animals to the composite makeup of the earth and the heavens, has been found precise, unerring in its composition. Scientists have discovered the formula, but that does nothing to explain origin. Science has no explanation for where it came from; they just confirm the reality of its existence. All else is labeled theory. Because the sciences rely primarily on mathematical equations and elemental formulas to substantiate its arguments, their errors are that they overlook, what is to me, the obvious - that both are the foundation of intentional design. It does seem a laborious process to dissect Order and look for random bits of truth that support a theory that somehow *something* has created itself from *nothing*.

It is not my intent to pick a fight with science, but when you dismiss its conclusions, I guess you do. Proverbs says, "Hope deferred makes the heart sick, but desire fulfilled is a tree of life." (Proverbs 13:12) Therein lies a big concern with the conclusions of science - hope deferred. Whereas God created and then set the worlds into motion, designed to perpetuate on absolutes and principles, science concludes random accidents. The seasons come and go with unerring precision, but the scientists cannot answer as to why that might be. It all leaves Mankind hanging in the gap between no beginning and no end, where's the hope in that?

In God, all things have meaning and purpose - and hope. And, for any who set themselves to look, Creation is confirmed in the midst of the formulas and equations. A man of faith, called to accept His Word without question, questions everything for in so doing he plumbs the depth of God in ways that will transform his soul, his life and all of the days that will be his portion. Yes, "...For now, we see in a mirror dimly..." (1 Corinthians 13:12). No matter the strength, capability or intelligence of man, he is limited, seeing and understanding only in part; whereas God sees beginning to end. Although the finite mind numbers a formula or a day, it was the Creator of elements and days that put them in order and gave them a plan and a purpose - and hope.

Hope records the birth of the promised Messiah. Jesus of Nazareth, born in Bethlehem and of the house of David was received and affirmed by wise and godly men as Messiah, the Christ. Predicted by Scripture, confirmed by history, we are not without enough discernment to know that God's purposeful and consistent design carries a message to those who would observe, even await the season He will come again. The pattern found in Divine Order should not surprise nor confound any man. God, who established all things, uses them to reveal Himself, His plan and His purpose to those who seek Him.

Time, nor science, has diminished the need for a Savior and wise men still find His saving and transforming Grace. And, when on that promised day He splits the eastern sky with the glory of His coming, wise men shall rejoice; not out of surprised amazement, but out of certainty that the Promise, long-awaited, has been fulfilled.

Entangled in the Net

"It was for freedom that Christ set us free; therefore keep standing firm and do not be subject again to a yoke of slavery." (Galatians 5:1)

Though the private dreams held in the imaginations of children should not have boundaries which are dictated by anything other than love and security, the reality of many children is that life is not always loving and security only as safe as those who control the moment. By the time a child becomes an adult, few are left unscathed by some polarizing circumstance of life that leaves them marked with an indelible residue of memory. These memories have the potential to counsel their every thought and action as they move forward in life. Most, although it is they who bear the scar, did not earn it by their own choices or works, but by the hand of others. If different in any way, often when not different at all, children are teased, called names, bullied and threatened. It's cruel enough when one is the victim of other children, unimaginably so when an innocent learns through the shame and abuse that has come through the hands of a parent or caretaker. No matter their beginnings, the effect leaves behind a soul forever changed; the past becoming an evil counselor to their thoughts, and actions, which continually seeks to undermine their trust of man and God. The effects of our history may hide for many days, but at some undetermined point in time, the pain of it grows a voice and begins to speak. Eventually, they will face the choice to forgive or assess judgment.

I recently read an article about a Blue Whale off the coast of California who was found entangled in fishing net. Unable to free himself, tired and sluggish, his huge mass floated in exhausted helplessness. His arch nemesis had become not so much death as the entanglement which now held the key to death. Undelivered, his end was pretty much sealed; but he found his deliverance through the hands of a team from Sea World who spent hours tirelessly cutting him free.

No one can live out their fullest potential from the counsel of a soul that remains entangled. Memory has a voice, its counsel always the same: you have a right to your hurt, to be mad, to be bitter. Whatever lies in the heart will eventually make its way to the lips, the fruit of our words then turning on us, becoming a self-fulfilling prophecy. I think it easier to repent of sins that are our own than to repent for feelings and attitudes about those who have sinned against us. The down-side of withholding forgiveness is that when we judge another guilty - even if they are guilty - that judgment ties us to that person/place/event as effectively as any whale that ever found himself tangled in a net. Our nemesis will have become not so much what happened as the entanglement we will not, or feel we cannot cut free.

Try reading the book of Matthew, in particular, the words written in red – that which Jesus spoke. The God/Man lives from those pages, telling of a hope and a future; one affirmed through the picture of how Jesus saw Himself and others, what He had to say about Himself and the humanity that sought Him out. He walked right into their messy lives, rarely separated Himself, and then only to pray. Jesus was never unsettled or undone by the condition of the heart of man, or the pain of an entangled soul. He met each one right where they lived; never walked away, considered their sin too much to forgive or their entanglements with life too much to redeem – they only had or reach out to seek Him!

Although nothing is written of his growing up years, they were lived as part of a family, neighborhood, and town; then spent His life walking with the very ones He would soon give His life to redeem. Living in community leaves little illusion about Mankind - that he can soar with the eagles or root with the hogs. The God/ Man grew in their midst, knew their scars, their joys, and sorrows, the struggles and victories from whence they had sprung.

I think only a Savior who had walked among the suffering could save them from it.

No one can undo the past or change what it wrote upon their soul, but in Christ, we are not without choices as to what to do with it. "So if the Son makes you free, you will be free indeed." (John 8:36) Planted in Him, the power of the past is stripped of its voice to speak accusation; we are forgiven and redeemed. He will always make the most of our choice - but we are responsible for making it. That's the ultimate truth of the liberty that rests in Jesus Christ; personal responsibility and knowing what to pick up and what to lay down - and where to lay it. When entanglements are about those things done to us, our responsibility lies in where we choose to let them live – or die. We are all Blue Whales who long to be cut free of the …yoke of bondage that so easily entangle us.

What Was I Talking About

"Who is this that hides counsel without knowledge? Therefore, I have declared that which I did not understand, things too wonderful for me, which I did not know." (Job 42:3)

I doubt that I'd stand alone if I confessed there are parts of the book of Job that I find troubling. I'm not sure why I am drawn to think about it these days; perhaps because there is much to be gleaned from its pages. To say there is a lot I do not understand would be accurate and more that I wonder over. Not because I would be so bold as to question that God has His reasons for every move, every chapter holding some critical truth I need; it's more truthful to say that my finite mind struggles to dig out precisely what the message to my life might be. I wonder at the message behind the accusation Satan made to God against Job; not so much that Satan accused, for that's what he does, but that God took the challenge, that's not typically what He does.

Knowing we are His creation and He can do as He pleases with all that is His is not always a comfort when pondering the tribulation of Job. The ways of God are not always immediately evident to the ways of human thinking. We have no real knowledge of who He is beyond Scripture – and the message there must be interpreted to us by His Holy Spirit. He is our Source - if we hope to take away a revelation that would first break up the fallow ground of our heart, mind, soul, and flesh - if we are to be healed and restored to a productive field.

Sometimes I think this Truth is especially elusive to us American Christians. America has a vast storehouse of social resources that boggles the mind of many nations of the world, many who would consider themselves wealthy to have such a standard. Has such abundance made us lazy in our need of God's supply and apathetic in our declaration that He is all we need? Do we even view need on the same level? We may love being Americans, love our country and our home; feel blessed with such bounty. We cannot, however, maintain that illusion without considering how quickly things can change and that we'd better have more to draw on than what is in our stores, our banks or what appears to be the unending supply of electricity, water, and food that runs into our homes.

Perhaps that is the most basic message of Job: if everything was stripped away, would God be enough? Most of us, I included, can only hope so. We're not sure and find the thought of it a little unsettling. We sometimes talk about how we'd like life to be a little simpler, not so hectic, but most likely what we mean is the hard places, the worry, the debt, the news of loss and pain that so often accompanies too frequent phone calls or the evening news. These things trouble our soul and make us wish God would do something; that He would sweep across our land and our world in revival, that He would fix all the pain, loss, war and insanity that has become the by-product of the ways and choices of sin. This world is a scary place at times for, if we look too closely, it threatens our peace, devours our children and batters our hope.

When life gets to be too much about us – our wants, needs, feelings, and problems – we find our self seemingly stuck, mired in an ever-thickening quagmire of self-made misery. Only when we set our faith and resolve to something (Some One) beyond ourselves are we able to release faith toward change and allow hope to be born. It does seem the best of us belongs to what we can give away, for in doing so we find our own needs and challenges met, with a sense of peace as its by-product. Possibly that is because in giving away we have created a vacuum into which His provision can flow.

It's hard to fault Job for the questions he asked and reactions he showed. Most of us would do as much, or worse, with far less loss. But ultimately Job's cries of despair and the questions gave way to revelation and repentance in Job 42 when he confesses (paraphrased): You can do what you want without being thwarted (see Job 42:2). I didn't know what I was talking about (see Job 42:3). All I knew about You was what I'd heard, now I...see...You! (see Job 42:4). I repent! (see Job 42:6).

In conclusion, the blessings of the latter days of Job's life were more blessed than his beginning days (see Job 42:12). But, perhaps the higher truth of Job was the faith-expanded way in which he saw, knew and trusted in His God. If that were to be the underlying purpose of every trial in our life, it gives new meaning to the Word of the Lord when He says, "Always giving thanks for all things in the name of our Lord Jesus Christ to God, even the Father." (Ephesians 5:20)

Taking the Leap

"Now the Lord is the Spirit, and where the Spirit of the Lord is, there is liberty." (2 Corinthians 3:17)

Although most find the concept of slavery nearly impossible to relate to, it is as old as recorded history, going back to at least 3500 B.C. It is spoken of in Scripture and endured up close and personal by the Israelites when slaves to the Egyptians. People sold their children into slavery for enough money to ensure survival for remaining family members; sometimes selling themselves into slavery for the same reasons. We shake our heads, not able to understand that a person might live their life in bondage or servitude, unable to make choices regarding their own life. Eventually, even the thoughts of a slave very likely belong to another. We would like to think that this concept belongs to the past, it does not; it is estimated around our world today between 25 and 40 million people live in some form of slavery; many of them children, often targeted for human trafficking and sex slaves. The innocent indeed rise to the top of the need for deliverance that exists because of this evil and insatiable lust for power and the greed that drives it, but this is only the tip of the iceberg that represents slavery.

We would prefer to think about the concept of liberty. It would not be so unusual that the one desiring it might often interpret it as *being free* – free of demands, free to make our own choices, free to think, to do and to be as we decide and when we decide. It is, however, a total misinterpretation to equate liberty with absolute freedom. As with any truth, liberty has cost, it has boundaries, and it has responsibilities; and does not exists outside them.

While slavery of the human body is more shocking, it is perhaps the slavery of the human heart and emotions that are more prevalent and more destructive when the subject is liberty; the soul of man the most considerable loss, for that is eternal. Jesus said, "I say to you, My friends, do not be afraid of those who kill the body and after that have no more that they can do." (Luke 12:4) That is an unsettling Truth. Liberty flies on the wings of eternity.

Only foolishness would think the flesh to be free; it is subject always to limitations, health and conditions; it tires, gets hungry, needs sleep and finally dies. Only the soul flies to freedom, and that because of the liberty with which Christ has set it free. It is the only real liberty we will know this side of death, this promised deliverance we "…keep standing firm in…" (see Galatians 5:1) and that is found through Christ alone. The soul who has set its trust in the flesh, a knee that refuses to kneel before Him and lips that will not confess Him as Lord and Savior, has not only lived their life in bondage, they died there.

Humans get so foxy, saying things like: my life is my own; I'll do what I want when I want. I belong to no one but me. That's never true, even in the farthest stretch of the imagination. If we are alive, we owe a debt and, although we do have choices, they eventually boil down to whom the debt shall be paid. Will it be the Lord Jesus Christ and the Blood He willingly shed for your sin and mine upon the Cross at Calvary – or the enemy that contests Him for the soul of every man or woman? Both souls are eternal, only those planted in Christ spend eternity in that place He has prepared for them. The more accurate reality, that which is eternal, lies in that which cannot be touched with the hand or seen with the eye. The greater battle each of us will ever know takes place in the unseen realms of the heavenly, that place where the spiritual forces of good - Jesus Christ - and evil – Satan - contest for the soul of each man. Men make up *religions,* hoping to quiet the cry of their soul, ever searching but never satisfied. They name it "fate" or "karma" and talk about it in quiet moments when that which is spiritual cannot be denied, often missing the nail-pierced hands stretched in invitation. The enemy of the soul of Mankind laughs, he does not, however, have the last laugh. Where the devil is sneaky, Christ is intentional. "…And the Lord was adding to their number day by day those who were being saved." (Acts 2:47b)

"But the Lord is faithful, and He will strengthen and protect you from the evil one." (2 Thessalonians 3:3) Once begun the process of Redemption, that moment by moment diligence that redeems every robbery and every loss, is on-going. It will take a while for the flesh and the emotions to find the liberty we seek. Not because Christ is slow to redeem, more because we have picked up a few habits and mind-sets while on the road of life. Although we may at times wish we had become a new creation in the immediate sense of the word, we appreciate the process of redemption a whole lot more when we can work out our salvation one deliverance at a time, to know His faithfulness, His love, and constant care. "But whenever a person turns to the Lord, the veil is taken away. Now the Lord is the Spirit, and where the Spirit of the Lord is, there is liberty." (2 Corinthians 3:16-17) Liberty flies on the wings of understanding. Many are the *veils* of man: sins, habits, false beliefs, attitudes, places where we have plainly missed the mark. Paul says their minds were hardened and the veil lies over their heart (see 2 Corinthians 3:14, 15) The Redemption of Jesus Christ is faithful, confronting each thing, large or small, that stands between Him and us. His Spirit is patient, awaiting that moment we agree to take the leap of faith, for He has removed every veil. Let us look that we might see – that we not remain slaves to our flesh but rest where the Spirit of the Lord is. There is liberty.

Peg Leg

"Then God said ... let birds fly above the earth in the open expanse of the heavens." (Genesis 1:20)

We live on a small lake and look forward to those re-occurring moments that accompany the spectacular variety of entertainment that migrating water-fowl brings. It is not unusual, here in the heartland of Iowa to have Pelicans, Sea Gulls and a wide range of ducks to stop by to rest before continuing their trek north, only to return south in the Fall.

This year we had two pairs of Canadian geese that stopped by and decided to stay. They nested and raised their young before us. By the time they looked to be adults, the two separate families had become one. We happened to be present the day the flying lessons began and watched with great interest and humor at the flapping and squawking rush across the water that often ended in either collision or cartwheel. It took a while, but all eventually made it airborne – save one. Whether hatched with one leg or subject to a turtle or other danger he had, to this point, managed quite nicely. He did have a slight tendency to swim in circles, but other than that small bent, he kept up with his gosling siblings quite nicely. But this latest development in their life lessons was beyond his immediate capabilities, and he remained alone on the surface of the water. The others practiced their new-found liberty, taking off, landing and then doing it all again. Each time they'd do a little better and fly a bit farther. When they returned from their airborne excursions, they would gather in a group, squawking and excited. More and more he was excluded, swimming alone in his ever-widening circles.

We watched with great sadness the day they all took to the air in what was a final flight and did not return.

Although he had tried valiantly to accompany them, this one was left behind. Days passed to a month. Jerry named him "Peg-leg," and we became protective and deeply touched by his lonesome existence and mournful call. He was genuinely alone the day a large flock circled and honked their way to landing. They were there a couple of days and gone one morning when we arose. We spoke of the sorrow we imagined that Peg-leg must feel at being left behind once more, but when we looked, we could not find him. We had not seen the triumphant scurry his one leg must have made across the water until his strong wings took flight, but we rejoiced as we imagined the feeling of elation that must have filled his feathered breast as he lifted skyward, unencumbered. His handicap had not written his end. He was not incapable – he had just needed a little more time. We miss him, actually; but would not for one moment deny him the joy of having overcome the limitation circumstances had laid upon him.

I don't think we would have enjoyed the saga of Peg-leg quite so much if he had not overcome the limitation life had settled upon him and taken to flight. He would not have survived our Iowa winter with one leg and no immediate source of food.

We humans especially rejoice when the underdog overcomes. Most likely that is because somewhere, somehow, we identify with what it's like to face life and circumstances alone or struggle to overcome some seen or unseen arena of restriction, lack or handicap. No one escapes hardships, not really. We all have something that has visited our life, causing us to limp with limitation or angst. Some have learned to hide it behind a smile, busyness or a cause. Some marshal their disappointment, their defense an attitude worn like a badge that keeps others at arm's length. Others give way to hate or violence that cries of their frustration, hiding the pain that accompanies their lack.

But, some have learned to use it as a springboard toward what they were born to do – fly. Good job, Peg-Leg!

Building the Wall

"Can a woman forget her nursing child and have no compassion on the son of her womb? Even these may forget, but I will not forget you. Behold I have inscribed you on the palms of my hands; your walls are continually before me…Lift up your eyes and look around." (Isaiah 49:15, 16, 18a)

I am both humbled and completed by the knowledge that my God knows me intimately – loves me well and has written me on the palms of His hands. He does not give the specifics that my curious mind wonders over: precisely what has He written there; a picture or name, my purpose or provision? It doesn't matter, what matters is that everything having to do with me is close and personal to Him. When I keep my hand in His, I stay aware of the inscription written there, knowing its indelible decree; only when I pull my hand away am I filled with wondering where He had gone. He misses no detail; my walls are continually before Him.

In the days of Isaiah, walls were the most critical protection any city had to offer. They not only defined the perimeter of that encampment, but provided security from the enemy without – enemies that were fierce and committed to destruction, unpredictable with their timing, but consistent in their threat. It was a lot easier to conquer a city from the inside, but a wise people didn't make it easy. Conquest required both the time and resources of an enemy before the walls could be breached, then razed; but this had been Jerusalem's fate, prophesied by the Lord and accomplished by the Babylonian king, Nebuchadnezzar. "Therefore thus says the Lord of hosts, 'Because you have not obeyed My words, behold, I will send for all the families of the north' declares the Lord, 'and I will send to Nebuchadnezzar king of Babylon, My servant, and will bring them against this land and against its inhabitants…and I will utterly destroy them…'" (Jeremiah 25:8-9) It was after some 70 years of captivity later that Nehemiah was commissioned by another Babylonian king, Artaxerxes, to oversee the rebuilding of the walls of Jerusalem. It was accomplished in an extraordinary 52 days under Nehemiah's watch as they carefully saw to the strength and integrity of each stone they laid. The primary motivation for the might of the walls probably came out of the fact these same builders lived within the shadow of the wall, its existence a hedge of protection that would keep them and their family safe, as well as the many others who lived within their circle of obedience to the Lord's commission.

I consider these *walls* an example depicting our life; the message here speaking a similarly powerful truth. We too have an enemy of our soul who does not wish us well, an enemy whose plan includes the battering of our faith, breaking down spiritual walls and breaching our spiritual hedge of protection. Our promised provision from the Lord is both given and kept under His care, unbroken in its consistency. If broken, it is we, by disobedience, apathy, or personal choices that have cracked the hedge of our protection, leaving ourselves uncovered and vulnerable. It is a sobering thought that we would uncover ourselves, through actions or attitudes, opening the door, making us vulnerable to attack. Good or bad, every choice has a consequence waiting on the other end of it. God's hand is not short that He cannot save, but deliverance and protection very much depend on us as well: what we give ourselves to or allow to cohabitate within: will we meet

Him in prayer, hide His Word in our heart seek His wisdom and follow Him in all of our ways? Because we are the ones who dwell within the protection of our *walls*, it would seem wise to tend to their strength and integrity. One whose name rests in God's palm has an unlimited resource for everything needed; but the choice to avail ourselves of His supply rests in our palm.

When He says that our walls are continually before Him, the spiritual interpretation, I think, must be this hedge of protection by which the wiles and plots of the enemy are kept at bay, rendering him unable to plunder our lives. No matter the measure of threat from without, we are safe within – if our walls remain intact. If we give ourselves to fits of anger, if pride or self-pity controls our choices, if we become overly attached to people, things, places or habits, we have cracked our hedge already. I guess anything that puts itself in even the smallest position of control over, or in, our life opens the door to destruction, allows the enemy to put his hand through the crack in our hedge.

It is well to remember that the safety found in spiritual walls very much depends on the cooperation and care we have given to the building and keeping of them. The Lord prepares us, leads us, and provides every resource; but He will neither force it upon us nor do it for us. It is our hands, heart, and obedience that set the stones He provides; those that we are well prepared to fit into our spiritual wall.

Whining is not a Gift of the Spirit

"God also testifying with them, both by signs and wonders and by various miracles and by gifts of the Holy Spirit according to His own will." (Hebrews 2:4)

I confess that I too often think about myself, how things affect me or make me feel, living as though the world revolved around me. Few of us will completely escape the challenges that accompany life, seasons of sorrow, disappointment or regret. I remember once whining to the Lord about why it always seemed to be me who had to wait for answers, why I had to be the one to change, sacrifice and deny myself. He quietly told me, "Because I asked you." I get some of my best answers following one of my *whine sessions* and usually not what I particularly wanted - but absolutely needed - to hear. Now, whining, although an unusual messenger, can prove a very enlightening one. It has a voice and a subtle message, expressed to any who would step back from the moment and let it speak. Whining often proves an excellent barometer for the deeper root of a problem; that often being: "I don't want to…," "It's too hard…," "Let someone else…." Most of us will, at some time or another, face a season of life where loss seems to be the rule of the day. Whining often goes a long way in exposing the sincerity of our heart regarding our depth of commitment to our part in accomplishing those things we've asked God to do for us or change in us - things such as putting our past to death or giving life to our future. What we whine about often serves as a spotlight, revealing those places where we need put on, put up, put off or just plain guard our heart.

Through the years I have prayed and claimed much for my life, my generations and those that stand as far as my prayers can reach. I find, however, that I must loosely hold even those most earnest prayers, leaving them, in large part, unexamined. To examine the process by which God chooses to work in the lives of those for whom we pray very often leads to frustration and disappointment if we were to observe too closely the path that answers sometimes take. We humans are an opinionated lot and we may surprise ourselves how quick we are to make observations, even giving God some suggestions – but perhaps I only speak for myself. One maintains faith by looking beyond what the moment currently holds and leaving the timing and the outcome in the hands of God; and that most often means waiting.

Since waiting will inevitably accompany our seasons of life, it becomes especially important that we not misinterpret these moments, or give them more power or attention than they are due. The waiting does not tell the whole of those whose life is kept by what I shall call, *the eye of faith*. No matter how fragile our flesh, nor fickle our resolve, it is the eye of faith that sees through to the other side of that which, for a moment, causes unrest for the one who waits. Faith looks to the Promise, to the One who gave the Promise, and does not leave the future in the hands of the moment.

Sometimes in the process of waiting, the vital things of our heart become groaning; the kind that issues forth from the depths of our soul - sometimes. We all hold unanswered prayers in the depth of our being, the greatest of those being for people we love and for whom we desire so much, lost people. At times we will see, hear and know too much that seeks to undermine our faith and challenge our peace, and our emotional hope gets rocky. We will all know a season - or seasons - of life where our spirit grows weary and our flesh weak when we wonder if God knows, hears, or will answer our heart; and our flesh whines its discontent. It's an outer expression of a spirit that hopes – waits – and does not begin to tell the whole of the eternal story. Some things are so important that words are not sufficient for the heart to express its deepest desires, so the spirit groans its hope.

We need not think Jesus would not understand or give Himself to a heart that yearns for Redemption and understanding to fall upon those He loves before the hour passes, and it is too late. "When He approached Jerusalem, He saw the city and wept over it, saying, 'If you had known in this day, even you, the things which make for peace! But now they have been hidden from your eyes. For the days will come upon you…'" (Luke 19:42, 43a). Jesus knew what lay at the end of His journey – for Himself, for the city, for the future of Mankind – and He kept the course, without wavering. As He looked beyond Jerusalem to Calvary, do you think perhaps He saw the face of each one of us standing in the long line that led to eternity, prayers in hand, hearts waiting?

Giving From a Meager Barrel

"For thus says the Lord God of Israel, The bowl of flour shall not be exhausted, nor shall the jar of oil be empty, until the day that the Lord sends rain on the face of the earth." (1 Kings 17:14)

Wisdom is, without doubt, worthy of the time any man would spend pursuing her. She is best esteemed, however, when accompanied by her sister, Understanding. Seeking both, Solomon spent his life sifting for pearls, stringing each hard-won revelation into the collection we know as Proverbs. Job, from the depths of his loss, the abyss of his despair, cried out for their balm and found them not to be lacking. Their ointment soothed him in his time of trouble and made way for the path that ended in revelation, restoration, and hope, albeit slowly revealed.

I think wisdom and understanding to be elusive to all of us unless the Holy Spirit of the Living God reveals them in and to us. They are fickle when left to the meager comprehension of mortal man for they do not walk at man's command or come to his bidding. They are merely the fragrance that accompanies His Spirit, and they fly softly to one who has set himself to know the Truths found buried between our seeking and His supply. It is in those moments that she comes, revealing the Truth of the ages to one who has set aside both pride and pre-conceived ideas, one who is eager to cast aside the chains that burden the soul.

No matter our level of experience, years of hard-gained wisdom, the gravity of the needs of those lives that revolve around our own often require more than we have to give - more resources, more insight, and wisdom. Those are the moments our hand dips into the barrel of the One who is our Provision for every occasion life holds; for us and those who look to us. It is then that we acknowledge with certainty, and a grateful heart, that because God has plucked us from the fire as a brand from the burning and revealed Himself to us, our lives have become a storehouse for Bread. Most of us enjoy sharing out of our abundance.

I wonder at the widow of Elijah's days of drought, the one who had but a handful of flour, a bit of oil and a few sticks left of her resources. "He (*Elijah*) called to her and said, 'Please bring me a piece of bread in your hand.' But she said, 'As the Lord your God lives, I have no bread…'" (see 1 Kings 17:10-16). One of the most difficult challenges of life revolves around a hand stretched forth to our barrel of resources that we find to be empty. Probably most of us could admit to having someone in our life that requires or asks more than we were willing or able to give from our meager store.

I have one such person in my life, one that prior shared experiences had depleted my supply. Regarding my history with them, I long ago settled those accounts with the Lord, so bear no feeling of un-forgiveness, but neither do I feel the emotions that seemingly should accompany such a relationship. I have prayerfully treated this dear one with honor and respect, often going out of my way to make sure I go the extra mile. It comes from a place that feels like a fulfilled obligation and that sometimes troubles me because there is no emotion attached and I often think there should be. But, we should honor because it is due, not because one feels like doing it. At times it's hard to maintain what *feels* like a fraud that borders on hypocrisy. It's then I acknowledge that we do some things because of obedience to a higher Truth.

It takes faith to reach our hand into the last of our meager resources and give them away, but that is the ingredient that causes the supply to remain consistent with the need. Elijah's widow never found resources that existed beyond the moments they were needed. Daily there was enough oil, enough flour to fill the immediate need at hand.

I was recently told by this person how much they appreciated my love and regard for them. It was surprising and humbling but carried with it a sense of revelation for which I had not expected or asked. I had merely been obedient - not my initial goal or purpose - and God had over-reached what I had unknowingly sacrificed and covered what had been a lack in me. I have many gaping holes of lack so have prayerfully come to count on His resources to fill that gaping space between my resources and the need.

The wisdom and understanding that come from the Holy Spirit over-reaches our bumbling inadequacy and covers our gaping wounds. We cannot think that feelings determine the measure of what we have to deal out to others; they are such a poor barometer of the truth of things. May we never withhold our hand because we did not feel like extending the gift. Freely we have received, now freely give.

A Balanced Life

"Let Him weigh me with accurate scales, and let God know my integrity." (Job 31:6)

On a recent venture to a Chinese restaurant, my husband found this saying in his cookie, "There is more to balance than not falling over." Now he didn't interpret these words as particularly profound; didn't reflect, ponder or look very far for a kernel of wisdom that might lay there. It is rare that one would spend much time considering those areas of life that are working well for them. Perhaps new revelations often begin as the need for a different perspective, as much as anything - at least that often seems to be the case with the beginning of them. Jerry's natural sense of balance is excellent, and he doesn't fall over as often as I. That's true in both his physical senses - he can ride a bike without hands on the handlebars - and spiritually as well - he doesn't tend to overthink. I'd fall flat if I removed my hands and I think way too much, often causing myself unnecessary challenges, I know. Perhaps overthinking would not be an entire exercise in futility if those of us engaging in it were to insist it take us to a conclusion. Which I have done: it is the balance of one's life that becomes the essential ingredient to one who seeks to live, spiritual as well as physical, without falling over.

Perhaps, if we can allow, there are many moments in the day to day of our lives that will either confirm the balance of our life and our faith or bring it into question. Balance is an ingredient that generates consistent forward momentum. Our lack of that truth initially presented itself to us in those days when we first realized ourselves to be poor and in need of something that would move us from the quagmire that kept us stuck in life. It would come through the repentance, Truth, and Redemption that would redeem our lives and bring restoration. We could not have known what it would mean when the Life of Jesus Christ within us would begin to balance flexibility with purpose; resolve with rest, need with a provision, spiritual principles with holiness, revelations with faith and faith with works. Apart from Him who is the Giver of Life, even the best of life cannot exist by itself for long.

It seems humans do better when challenged. Give us a life of ease with nothing left to conquer and apathy and laziness soon become our intimate partners. Let us remember that spring day when David decided to stay home when the kings went out to battle (see 2 Samuel 11:1). "Now when evening came David arose from his bed and walked around on the roof...saw a woman bathing; and the woman was very beautiful..." (2 Samuel 11:2)

We could conclude that David had lost balance in his life that day he sent another to do his job. It's nice to have people who will intercede or do for us, but they are no replacement for what God requires of us. Bathsheba was a big detour in David's life, his sin with her keeping him from one of the greatest desires of his life: to build the Temple of the Most High God in Jerusalem. That would now fall to his son, Solomon. God didn't revoke His Promise to David, for Jesus will always be of the House of David, but David did pay an enormous personal debt for his choices. Yes, there's a whole lot more to balance than not falling over.

David did not allow his failure to define the rest of his life or his reign. Although he would never build the Temple, Israel prospered economically under David, militarily becoming a force to be reckoned with as well. The balance of God's chosen people has always hung on their relationship to Him. When they walked in His ways, the people prospered. When they turned to their resources, God lifted His hand of provision and gave them to their own choices: that's balance. For good or ill, every decision bears with it an effect. Let us not forget that because of the shed Blood of Jesus Christ, those of us who call Him by Name are God's chosen people and our choices always matter.

Here are 7 points to a balanced life:

- Cease asking others about what they think you should do – set yourself to seek and know Him through His Word and prayer and then listen to what He says.
- Don't be so concerned with yourself – at times everyone feels insecure, lonely, or fearful. It does not last, neither does it define you.
- Alleviate much of your lack by reaching out to fill the need of others.
- Don't try so hard to avoid a challenge, change or commitment; practice facing what comes when it comes.
- Speak words that encourage and bless. If you can't do so, hold your tongue.
- Know God is faithful to perform His Word in a complete and timely manner - and we really can wait for His best.
- Learn to laugh – life is much too serious to live it without levity.

Rise to the Vision

"Then the Lord said to me, 'You have seen well, for I am watching over My word to perform it.'" (Jeremiah 1:12)

In the previous verse, the Lord had asked Jeremiah, "...What do you see, Jeremiah?" (Jeremiah 1:11). When Jeremiah answered what he saw, the Lord responded that he had "...seen well for I am watching over my word to perform it."

Jeremiah, often referred to as the "Weeping Prophet," lived from about 627 to 580 B.C. prophesying to people who had fallen far from the life of holiness the Lord God asked of them. He served during the time leading up to and through the destruction of Solomon's temple, and the end of the kingdom of Judah when the Babylonians took the cream of Judean society into captivity. Watching the formation of history was borne most heavily by Jeremiah, the one who knew what was to come, but saw his warnings go unheeded as he lived to watch it happen. Though his life was lonely and full of sorrow, Jeremiah's constant message was one of faith in God even in times of great affliction.

God's plan is both eternal and absolute; it does not rise or fall according to the triumphs or failings of man. If God makes it known through prophecy and His Word confirms it, He will give direction and make known to us what part is ours to do or to be. As for Jeremiah the Prophet; His word was to a nation – God's chosen people, the one through whom the promised Messiah was foretold and fulfilled. It would not come to this disobedient generation; for their wicked ways, they would eat the fruit of bondage and slavery before they would know repentance and deliverance.

Though life has drastically changed from the days of Jeremiah, God is the same. Why would we dismiss the reality that He still sends prophets to walk among us, sit beside us at church, work with us, speak and preach to us or live in our homes? Webster says a prophet is: One who utters divinely inspired revelation. Does the God of all Creation still desire to speak, lead and encourage His children? Absolutely! The Holy Spirit has not suddenly been struck dumb, He is alive. "For the eyes of the Lord move to and fro throughout the earth that He may strongly support those who heart is completely His..." (2 Chronicles 16:9a). It is He who reveals the truth of the Word, giving understanding where none dwelt a moment before, reveals provision we did not see, confirms a path to follow when the way is unclear. A prophet of the Lord is one who speaks a word of Truth that God lays upon his heart and spirit, one who speaks encouragement of days and a life beyond the moment, or plants hope where none exists.

Paul says, "For to one is given the word of wisdom through the Spirit, and to another the word of knowledge according to the same Spirit." (1 Corinthians 12:8) When someone has a word of wisdom - speaking biblical truth with clarity and understanding - or word of knowledge - knowing and relating what the Holy Spirit revealed - we should not consider it unusual that He would bring another before us for prayer or a word fitly spoken. We are, after all, His ministers. Neither should we be surprised that He would give specific insights, that through our prayer and counsel another might be encouraged, corrected or find an answer or direction they'd long sought.

If you are either giver or recipient of such spiritual insight, a simple litmus test of credibility lies with how it lines up with Scripture. A prophecy never consists of words snatched out of some invisible place; it cannot add to, take away, or make promises apart from what God has already spoken. If any word given is not compatible with Scripture, dismiss it as coming from one that was probably well-meaning but mistaken. And, if what was spoken lines up scripturally, but you don't understand? Seek Him for understanding and direction before you take it to heart or act upon it. He will give revelation; for He works according to a plan fit perfectly to you and never rushes you to do something before it is time. Our God is Spirit, alive but unseen. It takes an ear to hear, and a spirit attuned what He would say - and that requires time and practice to perfect. "I thank my God … for the grace of God which was given you in Christ Jesus, that in everything you were enriched in Him, in all speech and all knowledge…so that you are not lacking in any gift, awaiting eagerly the revelation of our Lord Jesus Christ." (1 Corinthians 1:4a, 5, 7)

When a true prophet of God speaks into our lives, we are encouraged and challenged toward change or growth; trusting Him for what our future days will hold. It may take weeks or years for His plan to be accomplished in us. If we are wise enough to rise to the vision, we will cooperate with and prepare our self for the provision set in store for us by God's hand, provided and specifically fit to those of us who set our ear to hear Him.

Filled With Power

"Fixing our eyes on Jesus, the author, and perfecter of faith, who for the joy set before Him endured the cross, despising the shame, and has sat down at the right hand of the throne of God." (Hebrews 12:2)

Oh my, how the devil danced when Jesus Christ hung upon the Cross. I imagine the hordes of evil watched, greedy eyes awaiting that final moment when death proclaimed its victory. It did look like they'd won. Every part of the Crucifixion seemed to fly in the face of the words He had spoken, the miracles, healings and the Promises He had made. Matthew says, "And those passing by were hurling abuse at Him, wagging their heads." (Matthew 27:39) With mocking scorn, they cast His preaching from hearts so recently penitent, and denying the words of His Promise, spat them back at the Lord of glory. To the music of their discord, the devil danced.

There is little of the whole of God's Plan that we humans genuinely see or entirely comprehend, and most of what we do see is only in part, it seems. Even with the help of the Holy Spirit our mind often feels dense and unable to grasp His intent, to comprehend the whole of Him, this omniscient God. And that He would plant eternity within this cracked vessel in which we dwell eludes our small ability to understand that He would, and for no other reason than love. Perhaps Paul felt similarly lacking in clarity when he said, "For now we see in a mirror dimly…" (see 1 Corinthians 13:12a). No one could know the whole, the scope or the intent of the Father's plan. Death, having always had the final say, stood puffed up and ready to claim his prize as Jesus breathed His last at Calvary.

The reality of those moments lay hidden beneath the agony of pain as Jesus poured out His life on the Cross in obedience to the Father's will. According to the Apostle John, these were last words Jesus spoke in those final moments, "It is finished!" (John 19:30) He bowed His head and gave up His spirit and darkness came upon the land, the veil of the temple tore in two from top to bottom, the earth shook, rocks split and tombs opened as the saints which slept in Him were raised to life (see Matthew 27:51, 52).

One can only imagine that moment when Satan realized it was he who had opened the door to his destruction. He surely thought that he had taken, when it was Jesus that had willingly given. Fury surely stomped his rage as he watched the door to eternal life swing open and the sting of sin and death submitted to the authority of His shed Blood. Having done all, won all, Jesus sat down at the right hand of the Father, leaving the authority of all He had accomplished in the hands of His disciples. The transfer was not sudden; He had been teaching them for many days, saying they would do greater works than He, "…because I go to the Father" (see John 14:12b). But, they did not understand.

It is true that Lucifer – Satan - is an angel cast to earth because of his pride and desire for authority (see Isaiah 14:12-21) but I found no Scripture that confirms that he has *authority*. The closest I came to a compatible concept was in Genesis where Adam was given dominion over the earth, and he gave over what was his at the serpent's suggestion. Matthew plainly says, "…All authority has been given to Me (Jesus) in heaven and on earth." (Matthew 28:18b)

I used to be afraid of the devil. I have learned that who I need to fear is me, lest I give away what is mine. Satan has no authority to take from me; only I can give him what God gave as my portion and my gift. No matter how loudly he roars, that lion has been rendered toothless (see 1 Peter 5:8). However, because I am no longer afraid of him does not mean I think it wise to taunt him. I would not presume upon God's Grace and assume it prudent to do so. Better that we keep our eyes on Jesus Christ, who won it all and set His authority in the hands of any who would stand in the gap between Heaven and earth. Jesus was never afraid, neither did He ignore evil, just stated, "Behold, I have given you authority to tread upon serpents and scorpions, and over all the power of the enemy, and nothing shall injure you. Nevertheless do not rejoice in this, that the spirits are subject to you, but rejoice that your names are recorded in heaven." (Luke 10:19, 20). "Behold," is used when we are asked to pay particular attention!

Our calling is to deny ourselves, learn about Him and then walk in all He accomplished. Filled with His power and presence, we walk beneath His authority and blessing; to bind and to loose, to operate in the gifts of the Spirit and to bear fruit.

Stitch, Stitch

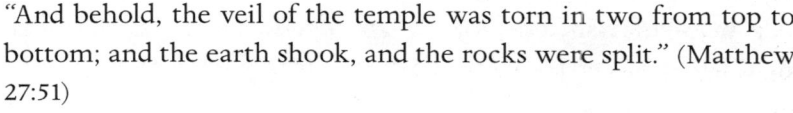

"And behold, the veil of the temple was torn in two from top to bottom; and the earth shook, and the rocks were split." (Matthew 27:51)

We don't always anticipate or choose the people or the moments that will shape our lives or define our existence. With most of us, we could point to certain scars on our soul; relive the hurt or loss with unerring precision, giving memories a fresh dose of energy and permission to counsel the moments of the day before us right now. "So do not worry about tomorrow; for tomorrow will care for itself. Each day has enough trouble of its own." (Matthew 6:34)

I wonder if Jesus considered the trouble the day would hold when He met the rising sun of the day that would redeem eternity; the day my sin/your sin was laid upon Him, and He bore it to the Cross? The day passed, and the people watched and waited; measuring, judging the moments and the man, they hurled their insults and laughed their doubt as darkness covered the earth. At 3:00 in the afternoon, "And Jesus cried out again with a loud voice, and yielded up His spirit. And behold, the veil of the temple was torn in two from top to bottom." (Matthew 27: 50, 51) With a moment in time, the purpose of God was fulfilled as He blessed the sacrifice of His Son, Jesus Christ, acknowledging it sufficient for the atonement of the sins of every man/woman who would believe on His Name and accept His sacrifice. God would never again dwell in the Holy of Holies; a temple made with hands.

Scripture confirms that when Jesus yielded up His Spirit, the veil, the barrier between God and man, was torn and no longer exists. Where once separation and Law had ruled, now reigned Grace, mercy, and favor, provision, purpose, and power, making all the promises of God, yes and Amen (see 2 Corinthians 1:20). How is it then, that we who are children of God, who have been made heirs together with Him who did and gave it all (see Romans 8:17), often live as impoverished debtors? Might it reflect the possibility that man tends to keep trying to sew up the tear in the veil?

We are called to walk in liberty, but rules often make us feel safer – stitch, stitch. I should forgive, but you don't know what they did – stitch, stitch. I can't; I won't, He couldn't – stitch, stitch, stitch. You get the idea of the subtlety with which we can once more be tempted to separate ourselves from the God who paid the price for our sinful lack with the Blood of His own Son. Anytime we think we cannot or He will not, to what avail is mercy, for we have chosen to stand aside from its redeeming flow. It may not be the most comfortable choice, probably not even the most natural choice, to deny ourselves the seeming right to feelings and offenses. Our flesh is insatiable in its demands for revenge, pity or vindication. It is a road widely traveled – stitch, stitch.

I well remember the day I knelt and asked Christ to forgive my sin and come into my life. It was a day that changed me forever, allowing me to slip from beneath the weight of all I had carried with me to that occasion. At that moment, so glad was I to be shed of it, I did not consider what the cost might have been. That revelation was for another day down the road, the day two missionary ladies visited our church and talked about sin. I knew about it, of course; I'd been saved from it, gratefully so. Until that evening, though,

I'd never been aware of the weight of my sin or what the price of paying for it had cost Him. Those moments of awareness crushed something deep within me, and I've never since been able to be casual about salvation or what it cost Him.

When Jesus shed His Blood, it removed every barrier, obstacle, and hindrance set between the God of all Creation and us. We may walk freely into His Presence with all our failings, foibles and fractures. It takes more than a moment to let that sink in. I don't know about you, but I'm tempted to think of my most celebrated lacks and most persistent flaws when I imagine myself standing in the presence of the Father – and yet He sees only the Blood of His Son and calls me *favored*. We are sons and saints, yet servants who must never forget the power that lays in repentance. Don't ever forget how to repent. Consider the need often, purposefully staying practiced.

The Blood of Jesus is not a blanket to cover our disobedience, our sin, our laziness, lack of discipline and desire not to be bothered or involved. The Blood of Jesus is first a beacon that casts light on the reality of our ways, nothing hidden and nothing distorted; next, a standard of holiness against which we may safely and confidently measure each act and attitude; then, a cleansing and faithful fountain whereby we may be made completely clean and whole.

Forever Lost in Him

"…If anyone wishes to come after Me, he must deny himself, and take up his cross and follow Me. For whoever wishes to save his life shall lose it, but whoever loses his life for My sake and the gospel's will save it." (Mark 8:34b, 35)

Although the writer of the Gospel of Mark, also referred to as John Mark, is accurate and specific to the life and words of Jesus, it is not because he heard them first hand. It's easy enough because his book stands in testament with those of Matthew, Luke, and John, to lump him in as one of the Twelve Disciples; he was not.

It is likely that he met Peter at the home of his mother, Mary, whose house had become one of many meeting places these new believers in Jesus Christ met for prayer and worship after the Crucifixion. He traveled with and became a faithful scribe for Peter, recording the heart, days and ministry of Jesus, as preached and seen through the eyes of Peter, whose life had been changed, along with the world as it had previously existed. Although Mark's days of ministry are most closely tied to Paul and his cousin, Barnabus, it was Peter's first-hand remembrances that live on the pages he penned.

We know little of Mark; his age or personal testimony of how he came to believe. He was a first-century believer, one who, having heard the Gospel of salvation in Jesus Christ, accepted Him as Lord and Savior. That he knew Christ in a personal and powerful way is testified to by the words that eternally live on the pages of his Gospel. Mark did have his own views, even an opinion regarding ministry; Paul speaks of this. According to Paul, he and Mark often disagreed; but again, on this Mark is curiously silent. Whatever the differences might have been, the more important message to take away from their sometimes rocky association is that disagreements and fractured relationships happen; and those too can be redeemed in Christ.

I wonder more at the heart of Mark as he listened to Peter. Hearing the Gospel did he believe, yet struggle to comprehend - not unlike we - the depth and personal meaning of the message? As Peter recounted the words of Jesus, "...If anyone wishes to come after Me, he must deny himself, and take up his cross and follow Me," (Mark 8:34b) did Mark count the cost? Did he ask Peter what he had thought when Jesus called him? Did he ask Peter if it was hard to leave everything behind and follow? Peter knew first hand, but this beginning of discipleship that followed the death and Resurrection of Jesus is curiously absent from the Gospel of Mark. He recounted Peter's testimony, his words, and view, discounting the temptation, perhaps, to state his own thoughts or the spiritual experiences that were his own. But these ponderings are only that; ponderings, the working of a curious mind, I suppose. For Mark had done as Peter had, denying himself, he left all and followed Him.

I am not confident that I entirely understand what it might mean to deny myself to follow Him. I can't say that my life planted in Christ has been that costly. Anything I've left behind seems to have held more destruction to my life than any value. Although not without challenge, His provision, wisdom, and hand of blessing on me has outweighed any cost to my often rebellious flesh; never ungrateful, but often rebellious. Perhaps that's the very thing I must deny within myself, that bent toward discouragement when an answer drags too slowly to the need, according to the dictates of my comfort zone anyway. Few of us shine our brightest in the waiting times. It is a cross I bear; this bent toward discouragement; one that often causes my hope to lag as I plead my case for a more immediate answer. Moments I give to despair are lost forever, my peace undone, my faith rattled. As surely as Christ bore His Cross to Calvary, there to redeem the sins of all Mankind; in kind, I must take up my cross and do the same, take that which undoes me to the place of redemption, there to be redeemed and restored by the Blood He shed on my behalf.

I do not see that redemption is a one-time prayer that saves the *all and all* of my soul. The prayer sealed the deal; my name there written in the Lamb's Book of Life, eternally. Redemption, the redeeming of my soul, has been an ongoing process as each unique and specific part of me; my gifts, talents, habits, attitudes, and bent, are tried and either redeemed - changed - or left to go another round - still struggling toward change. The more defined the natural tendency of my flesh the harder the challenge, but He doesn't give up on me. I don't give up on me either, for discouragement will not bind me or stop me from growing and moving with Him. I repent, pick up my faith and move on; I have no other Source. Bit by bit this life of the flesh is being lost in Him and laid upon the Cross – Redeemed!

Take Time to Plant

"Bless the Lord, O My soul, and all that is within me, bless His holy name. Bless the Lord, O my soul, and forget none of His benefits. Who pardons all your iniquities, Who heals all your diseases; Who redeems our life from the pit, Who crowns you with loving-kindness and compassion; Who satisfies your years with good things, so that your youth is renewed like the eagle." (Psalm 103:1-5)

"I'm bringing flower seeds to plant in the garden, GG" (Great Grandma), came her sweet voice over the phone. She was only going to stay for a couple of weeks so the flowers I would enjoy, would be savored alone.

It warms my heart that another generation is making their way to Iowa to spend a week or so. Her momma had done the same before her, though that seems so many days now past. Yes, the generations just keep growing and changing. Once, not so very long ago, it was I that was the young mom, and now I am old. My mother once told me that the years you look back upon were quickly spent. My youth could not comprehend what maturity now confirms.

David said, "As for man, his days are like grass, as a flower of the field, so he flourishes." (Psalm 103:15) The experiences of the days we are given upon this earth too soon confirm this Truth, or should, and this season was no exception; my days, those once green and verdant with youth and vitality, race ever more quickly toward the winter of my years.

She's bringing flower seeds. Dear child, she knows her GG's heart: planting. Oh, we will make a big production of the moment, taking with us a jar of lemonade to set in the shade, awaiting the rest we will take when our toil is complete. We will talk as we choose the perfect spot, as we till the soil and drop our seeds. I will gather her close to my heart and look into her young face and speak life and love, acceptance and affirmation. And the cares of her young being, which are too many in today's demanding world, can melt away for these moments spent in the sunshine planting seeds. Yes, her GG loves to plant!

The world is a busy place, offering an overwhelming abundance, almost too many, things to do and places to go. Parents, already burdened with jobs that are ever more demanding, do their best to race home to meet their self-imposed marathon of swimming lessons, ball practice, dance, music and a quick supper at the most convenient spot. Throw in a load of laundry and "hit the hay", hopefully, ready to do it all over again the next day. Life is busy, often too busy, leaving the time we spend as a family to those transitional moments left over as we race from one commitment to the next. Hoping all the exposure and experiences we provide for them will make them more well-rounded individuals, it is often at the expense of those personal and purposeful moments that build the foundation of their soul – those sitting in the shade with a glass of lemonade moments.

We are all born with our internal recorders already running. Our little *feelers* automatically know how to search about; to interpret our surroundings, what's being said and done and what that means to and about us. "Can I feel safe or do I need to be on guard?" "Am I wanted or do they think me an imposition or hardship?" Always casting about, our soul confirms the seed that is being planted there and predicts the crop that will one day be the harvest of this young life on the cusp of building internal values and self-worth.

At 75 years of age, I can still go to the garden which flourished under the warm Iowa sun and, for a moment, be that young girl who walked down the rows at her Grandma's side. I hear her voice, feel her close embrace and know approval and acceptance that completed a part of me. That child, that safe and secure young girl, still holds considerable influence over a demanding life and choices that are eternal.

I think it vital that we not let the quiet moments of life be a sacrifice to the busyness of one more activity or the demand put upon us by one more electronic device. A seed needs to rest in the sunshine – hopefully at the side of one who gives it permission to grow, to bring life and hope to our soul.

I hope you take time to plant …

Do Not Tickle My Ears

"Then He said to me, 'Son of man, stand on your feet that I may speak with you!' As He spoke to me the Spirit entered me and set me on my feet; and I heard Him speaking to me." (Ezekiel 2:1-2)

Anyone who would visit those Old Testament books written by a prophet of Israel (i.e., Jeremiah, Daniel, Ezekiel) might have some insight of what life was like for a people set apart to live in a land that was not their own. God's people of earlier days are not so very different than we "strangers and pilgrims" that also live in a land not our own. It is true that we have some that faithfully love and serve the Lord God and people who do not. That the one affects the whole of the land, the choices, laws and accepted standards found in that nation are valid concerns. Not every person that was carried forth from the country God had given them, to a life of captivity and bondage, was disobedient; not everyone had turned from Him. Some were faithful and remained so, even in the land that was not their own, but they walked in the same chains and felt the same lash; because the days were evil. Ungodly men may have chosen the different path, but it is one upon which the faithful would also walk.

I think about the future of our own country sometimes when I listen to the news and hear we can no longer have the Ten Commandments or the Nativity on public grounds, no prayer in schools, the controversy that often ends in changing laws and restrictions on liberty; but, I digress. For today let's keep our thoughts on those people who had already made that journey that took them from living in liberty to living in forced bondage. God's Word to them was to go ahead and live their lives, right there in the midst of that land that was not their own; to work, marry, have children and increase. To the Remnant, those who knew Him and called Him by Name, the purpose, promise and provision had not changed. He was with them wherever they were and whatever the circumstance of life around them.

Ezekiel was a young man when exiled to Babylonian slavery. He was both priest and prophet to a people reeling from what was the outcome of the season of the spiritual backsliding that had preceded it. Out of a sea of countless faces, the Lord looked into the face of one, Ezekiel, and spoke to him. He did not tickle his ears with vain platitudes, build his self-image, bolster his confidence or hide him from the troubles of the day; neither did he promise deliverance. Being young and inexperienced was no hindrance when God moved upon Ezekiel in chapter 1, showing him in a vision the breadth, life, and glory of the Lord God. When the vision closed, Ezekiel had a better understanding of the holiness and nature of the God he served. "And when I saw it, I fell on my face and heard a voice speaking."

Perhaps it is never any different when the call of God rests upon any man. One must encounter and know the One who calls before he can be equipped to serve with an undivided heart. In Ezekiel the Lord told him to "...stand upon your feet that I may speak with you." (Ezekiel 2:1b) The position of Ezekiel's body was a good reflection of the position of his heart: submission ("I fell on my face...") And commission ("...the Spirit entered me and set me on my feet," See Ezekiel 1:28b and 2:2). Ezekiel stood, and in so doing acknowledged: (1) God's authority (2) His right (3) his own willingness to the call (4) his authority to act on God's behalf.

The parallels in history should never be lost on us for if we do not learn from it, we are doomed to repeat it. Ezekiel lived his faith in the midst of a people God calls rebellious, stubborn and obstinate. That sounds similarly descriptive to the days in which we live. Can one man with an obedient and willing heart make a difference? It can when, "... the Spirit entered me and set me on my feet, and I heard Him speaking to me." God chose a man. He ordained a man. First came the vision, then the reality, followed by the power, wisdom, and resources to walk in all the Lord God asked of him. Obedience to God's revelation was the fulcrum upon which all future days balanced. In those moments Ezekiel acknowledged that the face and nature of God had eternal authority over evil and His hand was not short that it could not perform. God has not changed.

If He calls us to stand apart - and He has, each in varied ways - He begins by planting a vision of who He is - and that within the heart of His chosen. From that moment, let not one occasion be lost to us because we were afraid, nor hope dashed by a heart where no purpose is employed.

In A Nutshell

"Since you have in obedience to the truth purified your souls for a sincere love of the brethren, fervently love one another from the heart, for you have been born again not of seed which is perishable but imperishable, that is, through the living word of God." (1 Peter 1:22, 23)

Thinking back to the days that brought me to that moment I knelt and asked Christ to save my soul, I know that young woman could not have imagined the breadth and width of the path she had chosen. She could not have conceived of the commitment Christ had made to help her walk it or what it would indeed mean to have her soul redeemed. She could not yet know that the soul was the seat of her emotions, that vital place from which feelings, thoughts, and perceptions of life had sprung, or the choices she would make because of it. She could not know or understand how long her soul had gathered information, had processed the data that had formed her personality, her senses, reactions, and path. She only knew that whatever life-experiences had brought her to that moment, they were not working well.

It's no different for any of us. Unredeemed, the soul is a hard, at times impossible, task-master; keeping rest at bay because of an insatiable quest to find something that fulfills and satisfies. Even a soul redeemed cannot be left to its demands. Because past habits allowed the soul to dictate to the flesh, salvation does not automatically cause it to cease its claim on us. Habits - both flesh and emotion - have become so ingrained in us we are sorely tempted to accept them as normal. That they are not *normal* will become the life-long journey we call Redemption.

The soul is where we will work out our salvation, "...with fear and trembling" (see Philippians 2:12), bringing each emotion under His care. If we do not submit our soul to becoming like Him, those feelings that have always set the pace for our reactions in the flesh will continue to have their way with us and rule our choices. The soul attracts according to the greatest need that lies within it; it's sneaky but unable to hide for long what secretly lies within, what it loves, is familiar and, often, those things it fears as well. When we pander to our feelings, shore up our lack and give ourselves to the *fixing of flesh*, we bleed in kind. When we deny ourselves, give our heart to being and living like Him, life pokes us and He spurts out. It is not the plan of God that our lives be ruled or tormented by our flesh or emotions. Having paid the debt of all of our sin, I think He must wonder why we would remain a debtor to that which He has already marked paid.

Having been given the gift of free will, it should soon become apparent that whatever we submit our will to be and to do will lay the path on which we will walk going forward. Those things we give to the authority and care of Christ will change us into His likeness, albeit not in one swooping transformation. A will that allows its own devices to choose, however, has no purpose beyond itself. It will sacrifice its hope just to remain comfortable and in control. It is quick to argue that its life is its own – a dubious road on which to walk. Free will was never designed to render us isolated to a lonely path. Preferably, it is His gift, one He gave in the hope we would willingly choose His love, fellowship and the plan He has fit perfectly to us; the very thing that will complete and satisfy us. Only when He completes our soul will we know sufficient resources; enough for our own needs and adequate to deal out to others with abandon and abundance. In a nutshell:

- It is never what we see or think we know of a person that tells the truth of them.
- We are all born of corruptible (perishable) seed.
- We are reborn of incorruptible (imperishable) seed – the two cannot live in peace.
- Our soul is the battleground.
- Who we genuinely are is who we see/believe our self to be.
- Incorruptible seed will change us – must change us if we are to live in hope!
- Transformation is not made secure through one choice, but many.
- The process to become like Him is eternal.
- Jesus never saw Himself as separate from the Father; we are not separate either.
- Truth is first born in the heart and mind, a seed of revelation awaiting its planting.
- Time and perseverance makes revelation our own by the Spirit that dwells in us
- Face life honestly, always resolve what you can, as you can.
- The only way to resolve the corrupted in life is to replant with new Seed.
- He will lead us in steps of transformation that are consistent, intentional and purposeful.

Dig a Deep Well

"...Jesus stood and cried out, saying, 'If anyone is thirsty, let him come to Me and drink. He who believes in Me, as the Scripture said, From His innermost being will flow rivers of living water.'" (John 7:37b, 38)

I find it curious that our memory can seemingly drop some of what passes before it into the deep abyss of forgetfulness while some moments stand frozen in time, written with unerring precision upon the slate of our remembrance. One such occasion for me was a teaching on Abraham's well my Pastor's wife gave; the actual details of time and place long sifted away, only the vital Truth lingering to counsel my way: Dig a deep spiritual well, one that will satisfy the thirst of countless generations to come. I guess you could say that those desires I've prayerfully planted in Him and my seeds of faith have been broadened and defined by that one Truth as much or more than any other.

When God called the man He would one day name Abraham, the call meant leaving all that was familiar to him. "Now the Lord said to Abram, 'Go forth from your country...your relatives...your father's house, to the land which I will show you.'" (Genesis 12:1) This call does not seem unlike the words of Jesus in Matthew, "Then Jesus said to His disciples, 'If anyone wishes to come after

Me, he must deny himself, and take up his cross and follow Me.'" (Matthew 16:24)

God's promise to Abram went far beyond the days that would number his life: (1) I will make you a great nation. (2) I will bless you and make your name great. (3) You shall be a blessing. (4) I will bless those that bless you, curse those who curse you. (5) In you, all the families of the earth shall be blessed (see Genesis 12:2,3).

I wonder if Abram considered the Promise a curious thing for he was 75 years old and his wife was barren.

If you were to travel to Beersheba today, you would find a modern and bustling city planted in what is the last fertile piece of ground before the arid and unforgiving Negev Desert. You would also see an ancient well that the locals refer to as "The Well of Abraham." Although not documented or proven by recorded fact, it is accepted as such because it has always been there and called as such.

It was here by Beersheba, according to Scripture, that Abraham dug his most valuable asset: a deep well. Having traveled far and experienced much, as portrayed in these few chapters in Genesis, Abraham settled on these dry and dusty plains to carve out the foundation upon which the Promise would rest. Water immediately became the most vital commodity to the basic survival of man and beast in this dry and barren place where God would shape the life of this man to whom He had given His Promise. If one were to wonder, why Abraham, I think the most telling Scripture is found a few chapters later; "Then he *(Abraham)* believed in the Lord, and He reckoned it to him as righteousness." (Genesis 15:6) Such a simple approach to finding the will and purpose of God for your life causes me to consider that we often make the search more difficult than it needs to be.

If you were to let yourself go, your imagination could still take you to a well in the dry and barren land called Tel-Beersheba. There one could walk the ancient path of the life of Abraham; his journeys, and victories, even his lies and mistakes, through which God wove the fabric that yet clothes us with the very same Promise; to those who would choose to dwell beneath its mantle. There in the wilderness, Abraham dug a well – a deep well – one from whom countless generations have drunk and been satisfied.

It was another well at which Jesus first called Himself, "living water." It was at this place where He told the Samaritan woman, "But whoever drinks of the water I will give him shall never thirst; but the water that I will give him will become in him a well of water springing up to eternal life." (John 4:14) It is this very same well to which our hope is bound; this well springing up within each one who calls Him; Lord, Savior.

Let us purpose to dig it deep, this well of Living Water. Dig deep into prayer; dig deep into His Word, allowing the Holy Spirit to water the desert places that blow a dry wind against our hope, seeking to shrivel our faith. Allow the Living Water to flow, constant and sure, that countless generations would know and drink of its comfort and Promise. May it be said of those who follow in our way that "...they believed in the Lord and He reckoned it to them as righteousness." (Genesis 15:6) Let those of our generation say that the water served from our cup was neither meager nor spare; but bountiful and fresh from His presence; for the *land* in which we dwell is a dry and desert place and He provides the only well.

Well Equipped

"Beloved, do not be surprised at the fiery ordeal among you, which comes upon you for your testing, as though some strange thing were happening to you." (1 Peter 4:12)

Not often, but sometimes I find myself in a season of discouragement. It seems that the catalyst of this cycle, in my experience, is usually preceded by a real circumstance, most likely something that challenges my emotions, frustrates my faith, and is beyond my control. The sense that we have, or are *in control* is a wily culprit and will lay the groundwork for many seasons of despair if we don't learn early to cut it off at the pass. Usually, any detour of faith lasts only a few hours, but a minute spent in its presence is too long. It chafes my pride to admit I sometimes find myself lacking in sufficient grace; but then, even an ugly truth won't hide for long. Life is made up of joys and sorrows, trials and victories, suffering and Truth.

Peter says that we should not be surprised at those things of life which cause us suffering, the disappointments that ravage our soul, for they have come upon us "…for your testing…" and sharing in "…the sufferings of Christ" (see I Peter 4:13). Suffering is not usually a word we run toward with joy. A lot of the value we place on life experiences is measured not by how we perceive their value to us as much as how it affects us. When Peter says we should not be surprised at "the fiery ordeal which comes for your testing," we are more prone to equate it to the nagging challenges of everyday life, those things that irritate our soul and make our flesh uncomfortable. It would be a rare occasion that our minds would take the words "fiery ordeal" all the way to suffering. And yet, Peter does in the next verse, saying, "...but to the degree that you share in the sufferings of Christ, keep on rejoicing..." (1 Peter 4:13).

Seeing the words "sufferings" and "rejoicing" in the same sentence is enough to send most of us looking for a more comfortable spiritual Truth. Suffering is rarely a concept we seek out or embrace, equating it most often with the kind of pain, loss, and discomfort Jesus suffered on the Cross. That Calvary embodied the extreme of every painful agony is borne upon every word that day of deliverance held, but perhaps the more profound suffering had been faced before the sun ever met that morning.

"Then Jesus came with them to a place called Gethsemane..." (Matthew 26:36a). It was here Jesus faced what tomorrow would hold, where He endured the moments His "...soul was deeply grieved..." (See Matthew 26:38). He prayed, wrestled with His sagging flesh as it faced its struggle with obedience to the will and purpose of the Father. None of us will ever face the suffering of a Calvary; but we will all face the suffering of a Gethsemane, battling the temptation to preserve our soul from the discomfort transformation will bring and denying our self in obedience to the Father's will. "Keep watching and praying that you may not enter into temptation; the spirit is willing, but the flesh is weak." (Matthew 26:41)

I began my page with a paragraph on discouragement. As with most of us, it doesn't take many words before those things that cause our soul and flesh to suffer rise to the surface of our thoughts and conversation. These become our more prominent temptations; those areas where we "...keep watching and praying" because they too often accompany unnecessary suffering.

We are rarely in a position to control the events or trials that invades our lives and challenges our attitude, thinking, and faith. Peter said we shouldn't be surprised at them, but we often find ourselves rehearsing the hardship instead of looking for what it might teach us, how it might refine us or what purpose it holds. The little control we have in life is mostly about where we allow our heart and mind to dwell. What we have allowed ourselves to think upon in the days that come before an ordeal will eventually make its way into our faith and out of our mouth. When the real trials of life present themselves, where we spent our "Gethsemane" moments will prove the path we walk going forward.

Whether we will have trials is never the issue; instead, it is *when* we have them that our heart and spirit must prayerfully prepare to stand. Peter says their purpose is for our testing - and to what purpose? That is what the Father knows, and we will find out in the joyous and often challenging moments of what we call LIFE. The obedience Jesus had to the Father's will did not come on Friday; not during the scourging, the walk up Calvary's Hill, the nails or the Cross. The question of obedience was settled in the Garden, those moments when He asked to be released from the "cup" and answered "...not as I will, but as You will" when it was denied Him. (see Matthew 36:39). Although any decision toward obedience will be required of us in a moment, the path it takes will be the one groomed by prayer and practice in the days that preceded it.

Refresh Me

"For He was teaching them as one having authority, and not as their scribes." (Matthew 7:29)

I like that Jesus never minced words, never apologized or backed down about who He was and what He came to do; His every word and action always pointing to the Father's eternal plan for Redemption.

The religious leaders of the day didn't understand His message; I think because the Truth of it lay beyond the concept of the legalism they embraced by which they lived, that which established and maintained their prestige, social position and standing within the community. Many who followed him were the rebels of the day, their hope demanding a king who would deliver them from the slavish government of the Romans and their appointed pawns. Each of them seeking - and therefore seeing - Jesus from the confines and stilted perception of what their own need wanted Him to be. Even those who followed Jesus, living and ministering with Him in the day to day, were not particularly quick to catch on that His purpose lay only in small part toward the temporal; that even the meeting of temporary needs He did in the light of that which is eternal.

John recounted the miracles of Jesus in great detail. He tells of the great multitude that was now following Jesus, "...because they saw the signs which He was performing on those who were sick." (John 6:2) He healed, so those in need of healing sought after Him according to their own needs; few of them considering, I imagine, the possibility that anything more might lay beyond that single-minded resolve. Jesus crossed the Sea of Galilee – the people followed, but they were unprepared and could not see life beyond what they sought to gain from Him. Only a lad had thought it prudent to bring his lunch, five barley loaves, and two fish; which Jesus blessed and fed those 5,000 men. Belly full and satisfied, they followed Him yet again.

Did you ever consider what the questions those men must have had as they talked about His signs and wonders, healing, the loaves and fishes? Jesus was a total enigma to them. They only saw Him through the veil of the temporary, a convenience that met their present need. Jesus answered them and said, "Truly, truly, I say to you, you seek Me, not because you saw signs, but because you ate the loaves and were filled." (John 6:26) This portion of Scripture continued with, "Jesus said to them, 'I am the Bread of life; he who comes to Me will not hunger, and he who believes in Me will never thirst.'" (John 6:35) These were people who knew *about* God, knew a lifetime of hearing the miracle of the manna that had fed their forefathers.

Historically they comprehended the promise of provision, but considered it for another day, another need, another people or another time. They were hungry now, hungry beyond the depth of their belly, but could not grasp that Manna walked among them, opening the door to eternal life, thereby, making provision for the need of man on both sides of death.

Caught up in their bondage, they had no fulcrum on which to balance understanding that the Deliverer walked among them. But then, Jesus always meets us first at the point of our need. Knowledge would say, we were hungry and He fed us. Wisdom, however, says we were hungry, and He gave us Bread.

Having said all He came to say, having done all He came to do, Christ was crucified, arose from the dead, then met His disciples on the Sea of Galilee to share a breakfast of loaves and fishes, as He had, perhaps, done many times before. This time was different for He did not teach nor did He heal. He had completed all He came to do, save passing the mantle of His authority into the hands of those who would hear His call to "Tend my lambs." Once again saying, "…do you love me? …Shepherd my sheep" (see John 21:16, 17).

The Bread of Life left Himself in the hands of men to be dealt out to those who would hunger and thirst after righteousness. Knowing He has limited Himself to such cracked vessels such as we should give us pause to consider the manner in which we serve up this Bread of Life that dwells so faithfully within. Would He find our service joyful and bursting with life; half-baked or stale, even moldy crusts too long from the oven of His Presence? Oh, Lord! May it not be said of us!

The Tax Collectors Sonata

"But go and learn what this means: 'I desire compassion, and not sacrifice,' for I did not come to call the righteous, but sinners." (Matthew 9:13)

The day begins as a cold, gray morning where I live. There will be no sunrise today, no brilliant burst of light that promises warmth and sets the soul awash with a certain sense of unbidden hope. Hope appears hidden behind gray and uncertain clouds. I wonder how many of us could say the same.

I wonder if Matthew ever sat awaiting a sunrise that never came, commiserating over his lot in life. Hated, disdained, shunned and avoided; he had made his life-choices and was paying the cost of them. Matthew was a tax collector. In those days there were few more despised for the term "tax collector" was also synonymous with "cruel, greedy and dishonest." Each tax collector set the amount he determined to be collected from taxable individuals, paid Rome their required duty and kept the rest for himself. They were wealthy, hated and isolated, having only other tax collectors in their company; they were thought to be as undesirable as the beggar at the gate. Perhaps more so, because even pity was not a commodity the people bestowed upon them.

It was to this man that Jesus said, "...Follow Me!" (Matthew 9:9). Few of us are the tax collectors of our day, but all of us have stood on the other side of that door – the one where we knew ourselves to be lost, a sinner. Many still stand there, no doubt at times hearing the call, "Behold, I stand at the door and knock; if anyone hears My voice and opens the door, I will come in to him and will dine with him, and he with Me." (Revelation 3:20)

Once through the door most of us, I included, will find that the longer we walk in Christ, the fewer sinners with whom we have close contact. We get set in our ways, our thoughts and patterns; so intent on our personal growth, ministry and the requirements of life that we rarely take a moment to remember how lost being *lost* really feels. It is never a conscious decision that we stop eating with the "tax collectors" and "sinners," we are just subtly drawn away by the busyness and demands life will surely hold. Perhaps a better translation is that we are drawn away by our *self*. So, how do we then, as God's dear children, return to the place where we once again speak into a fallen world after we realize our voice is only singing to the choir?

Perhaps we begin close to home and work our way out from there.

To think that witnessing is only about telling someone that Jesus loves them, that He died to forgive their sins, is to miss the mark of the whole truth of what a witness is. Those occasions when only our mouth and heart do the talking are vital; they are also the easiest. It is the witness of our life, the day in and day out *voice* of what our life holds that speaks loudest to those with whom we live, work and co-exist. The testimony of our life is where the tire of our beliefs hits the road of godly reality. We are always witnesses. Whether we open our mouth or open our life, we witness every day according to what we believe about the Lord we serve, how intentional we are about whom He is, what He says and the integrity with which we live our relationship with Him. We cannot discount that the attitude with which we engage in life most likely speaks a louder and more truthful witness than the words we use.

The world holds God's people to a higher standard, often a standard of conduct that is higher than we have for ourselves. They expect us to be honest, our behavior to be above reproach, our word to be faithful and our actions to parallel our conversation. If it is not, they will call us on it – and they should. We ought to be held accountable and if we do not do it for ourselves, or for each other as brothers and sisters in Christ, then let the world remind us. If we seek to affect people for Christ, it must be because our life communicates that God's way is a better way and well worth the journey. We have nothing of lasting value to offer otherwise.

If we truly believe we are His inheritance, sons of light, saints, in authority, blessed, can do the impossible, are filled with the Holy Spirit and have eternal life, it is not unreasonable that we should live in such a manner that would consistently reflect our heritage. To live as whining, discouraged purveyors of dismay and gloom is a robbery; both to our testimony of faith, the evidence of who He is and the Word of Redemption He spoke concerning every man. Because we are His testimony, let us *preach* the Truth by our word and all we set our hand to be and to do, to be able to say to the Matthews of life, Follow me, I will show you the path to Life.

A Big Stretch

"And the earth was formless and void, and darkness was over the surface of the deep, and the Spirit of God was moving..." (Genesis 1:2)

My husband often teases me with one of my favorite sayings, "Everything has a place and should be in it." He says that is the epitaph that should be engraved on my tombstone and I guess it would be fitting. I do like order.

When I was younger I would fiercely protect the order of my home; but for a far different reason, I've realized. I used to be such a mess in my inner thoughts and emotions, they seemed so beyond my ability to discipline, the outward was all I could control, and I did so judiciously. Jerry used to say I was the only woman he knew who had her husband's socks washed and back in the drawer before they ever hit the floor at night. Now that is perhaps a bit of a humorous stretch, to be sure, but maybe not a huge one. I must have been hard to live with, being so unsure, fearful and driven.

Salvation and these years of God's Grace, His revelation, and deliverance, have tempered my obsessive compulsion toward control. Oh, I am still orderly in my home, yet believe everything has a place, but it's by choice, not to make up for some personal inner lack. It is amazing how different the same thing can look, depending on the source from which it springs. It indeed serves as a quick study on how quickly our flesh can pervert a principle.

God established His Creation through the principle of Divine Order. That is what keeps His worlds, and all that inhabits them, established at the dawn of Creation. The first few verses of Genesis say that out of that which was without form and void came order. The light separated from darkness, land from the seas, and heaven from earth. Everything had a place, and everything was in it. Then came animals of all types and various species – and, "Then God said, 'Let Us make man in Our image, according to Our likeness; and let them rule over the fish of the sea … the birds of the sky … the cattle and over all the earth …" (Genesis 1:26).

I find it profound and beyond my ability to completely comprehend the whole of what it might mean when He says that "Us" - Father, Son, and Holy Spirit - created each one of us in "Our" image. Not able to thoroughly grasp the infinite whole of it, I started at the only place a finite mind can: with a cursory study in Wikipedia about DNA (deoxyribonucleic acid), that molecule that encodes the genetic instructions used in the development and function of all living organisms. And the materials used for what must be a profoundly complicated formula? Elements – that "dust from the ground" we read about in Genesis 2:7.

I find it interesting that, although science can disassemble the elemental makeup of man to this degree of knowledge, the understanding of *how* still eludes them. Theories certainly exist; but, they remain beyond my mortal or emotional capabilities to entertain that all of Creation is some cosmic accident. We all know it is impossible to create something out of nothing - just try putting your breath to a handful of dust. But, if one were to use every known theoretical argument to explain that which is unexplainable, the intelligence of man comes up short, and the conclusion is that: There is much we simply do not know. I agree, but would argue that if one were to assume that if all we do know regarding creation were to have begun with even one molecule - as some have said - then who created that? It seems a more significant leap of unsupportable faith to relegate all I love and cherish to some cosmic accident than to a God who intentionally created out of love because He wanted some fellowship in the garden during the cool or the day.

I guess it boils down to a man's fundamental belief system; for most humans become adept at practicing the art of believing what they want to believe. Left to our thoughts, we can come up with an odd collage of beliefs and not require any of it to be supported by anything beyond, "That's what I believe." And, when they cannot prove God they conclude He does not exist? To me, the opposite is true, for when I look, everything I see confirms a purposeful and intentional Creator. To accept the precise order of DNA and the solar system to some "Big Bang" is too big a stretch for me, and does nothing to explain that something could come from nothing in the first place. But He who made it all, allows each to choose what they will believe while enjoying all of Creation in the process. Now and into eternity He has gifted us with free will, letting each one decide in what to dwell and, I think, where.

Hope, Hope, Hope

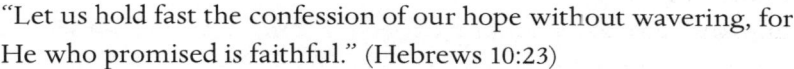

"Let us hold fast the confession of our hope without wavering, for He who promised is faithful." (Hebrews 10:23)

The morning was crisp, the breeze playing havoc with the leaves as I settled myself with my Bible, my notebook and a cup of coffee. I love new mornings, those few moments when quiet reigns. But then, there's a saying, "Plans are what we make so we'll have something to change when reality happens." A lot of life fits into that parameter. I had planned a quiet moment, but I slowly became aware that something had the dog unsettled and pacing in front of the fireplace. When I arose to investigate, I discovered a faint scratching coming from the firebox and a bird perched on the grate. So much for my coffee and quiet moments for suddenly, life was calling. I'm sure the bird was more frustrated than I. She'd put her hope in a dry, comfortable place to make a nest only to find nothing stable on which to build. Perhaps she should have been more careful about where she planted her hope.

We recently found ourselves as ears for a lady who was lonely. As we listened to the tale of a woman we didn't know about people we didn't know, it quickly became apparent that what we heard was what lay in the heart of one who hoped. She *hoped* her daughter would make good choices, *hoped* her son would stop being mad at her, *hoped* her mom's health - and so on. We had become an audience for her, "...hope deferred... "(see Proverbs 13:12).

It becomes easy enough to forget what life was like before we had a place in which to plant our hope. And, far too easy, in the busyness of our lives, to stop listening to the voice of a world that has no field in which to plant, other than the undefined and unplowed ground of their fragile wishes. That their present small plot has been over-run with the cares of life cannot be disputed. We could not answer the longing in her voice, but for God there go we. We know that our lives and our days would have been the same if we had not set our ears to hear something other than our despair, which had become a worn voice thin of hope.

I think the ability to hope is one of the most exceptional characteristics we humans enjoy. It is also our best possible resource for change. Good things spring forth from a hope planted in something more substantial than the grasping of incomplete and temporary resources.

The downside of hope is that it has no life within itself alone; it needs to be planted in something, someone - Some One - if it is to produce anything other than what it is – a seed awaiting the planting, a field in which it might rest. Hope, for its sake alone, is like casting one's seed to the wind. We were not designed to be the supplier of our own needs or the well of our hopes. Like the farmer, we plant and harvest but the seed was not of our making; nor can we cause it to grow. No matter how capable or gifted we are, our resources have limitations, our gifts restrictions. "Knowing that you were not redeemed with perishable things...but with the precious blood of a lamb unblemished and spotless, the blood of Christ...who through Him are believers in God, who raised Him from the dead and gave Him glory, so that your faith and hope are in God." (1 Peter 1:18, 19, 21)

The life for which we hope and the desires of our heart are in the seed; IF it is prayerfully planted in the field of Jesus Christ and left there, waiting the day of harvest. Each of us, having been born within the plan and purpose of God our Creator, will eventually run to the end of our self. At that point, we either realize we need a Source beyond our self, or we begin to borrow from someone or something to shore up our poverty of spirit, hoping to keep some semblance of significance and, hopefully, control. Our flesh-nature instinct demands self-preservation, and yet we are not our own. Christ bought our liberty, paid the price that remains beyond our comprehension. His willing sacrifice on our behalf constrains us to cease living as one who has no hope. Stay engaged in life. It's messy to stay involved with people and easy enough to cease being ears to the lonely and bread to the hungry. The danger of that excuse is that, although alive, we have quit living. Regardless of age, no matter the years of selfless service: it is a death sentence to cease being actively engaged in something or someone beyond ourselves. We need to risk being the ears that hear every bit as much as the one who takes the risk of being heard. If we are to remain alive; radiantly, expectantly alive, it must be that we live for a purpose beyond ourselves; and that never changes. "Let us hold fast to the confession of our hope without wavering, for He who promised is faithful." (Hebrews 10:23) Amen!

The Wings of Redemption

"Rejoice always; pray without ceasing; in everything give thanks… Do not quench the Spirit; do not despise prophetic utterances. But examine everything carefully; hold fast to what is good; abstain from evil. Now may the God of peace Himself sanctify you entirely; and may your spirit, soul, and body be preserved complete without blame at the coming of our Lord Jesus Christ. (1 Thessalonians 5:16-23)

Paul lays out here a comprehensive study of a life lived in Christ, concluding with the hope that in Jesus Christ our spirit, soul, and body be preserved complete at His coming. Since we don't have any way of knowing when that might be; the better attitude toward a life lived in Christ should be to live in a state that is ready for any day or any hour. John says, "Now, little children, abide in Him, so that when he appears, we may have confidence and not shrink away from Him in shame at his coming." (I John 2:28) The body returns to the dust of the earth, the spirit will return to Him who gave it (see Ecclesiastes 12:7); leaving our soul standing the most significant risk of being ill-prepared. The soul is the essence of who each one of us is created to be; complete in its unique individualism; it is the seat of our gifts, emotions, personality, and will. It is also the spiritual part of us, perfectly fit to know God and to hear His voice, it provides the throne – the position from which our life will be ruled. The choice of who will reign from there remains with us. The soul will either keep us in touch and aware of Christ and the process of spiritual redemption regarding those things which separate us from God and His ways – or, in touch with our feelings, needs and perceptions. A wise man will allow Christ, Savior and Redeemer, the honored position; but wisdom is hard-won, and often defers to the arguments our flesh and emotions make.

It is not unusual to find people who know and have served the Lord for many years still given to periodic spells of depression, dark spiritual moods or prevailing sin. It seems incompatible that such opposing concepts could continue to dwell within the confines of one heart; but perhaps not. What we give ourselves to after Redemption by the Blood of Jesus Christ is probably more important than what we gave ourselves to before. All things, good and evil, stand upon the foundation of choices we make and what we allow to live within our soul. We cannot continue to dabble in fear, judgment, prejudice, sin, and self-condemnation, and expect to reap a harvest of peace, stability, and balance. His Blood paid the price for the one, so we can live in the other. Proverbs counsels us to "Watch over your heart with all diligence, for from it flow the springs of life." (Proverbs 4:23) I interpret that as meaning we need to keep a short list with what lays within our heart – soul - for it is certain that our lips will eventually say whatever thoughts we harbor there. Let us guard the fruit of our lips, lest they speak a self-fulfilling prophecy.

As surely as the battle of good and evil lives so lives the battle between the flesh and the soul of every man. The open door through which we maintain the balance of power always begins at the Cross with repentance; and confession is its servant.

One of my dearest friends died young, leaving a hole in many of our lives; but more significant was the legacy she left us. Her personality was fiery and engaging. She loved to laugh, to cry with equal abandon, sometimes doing both in the same conversation. I loved her, but what I enjoyed most was to hear her pray. Because of her genuine honesty, she never gave the Lord excuses for her failings. She was quick to take responsibility for her choices if they had been unwise, rejoicing just as quickly for the answers and the blessings. She was not one bit shy about letting her requests be made known to Him. She was not perfect in her pursuit of God, far from it she would have told you, but did not worry about the state of her soul because she kept such short accounts with God. To this day I cannot hear the word, "faithful" without thinking of my friend, Anna, for I so often heard her pray, "Lord, I call your Name, Faithful." I think she did not count or measure the value of her life by the struggles or the failings, which were many. Instead, by acknowledging He'd been there through all of them, sustaining her and teaching her, boxing her ears when she needed it; loving her through it all. As I said, she was always honest with God, never sugar-coating or explaining away her less than perfect life or actions, yet rejoicing with great abandon.

Once our soul takes flight upon the wings of Redemption there are no limits to our destination; only the Lord knows our days from beginning to end. He has made "prophetic utterances" through every Promise written in the Book. Whether reminded by the words of another in your ear, by your reading, or the soft voice of the Holy Spirit as He speaks life into your soul; "Do not quench the Spirit, do not despise prophetic utterances. But examine everything carefully; hold fast to what is good...Faithful is He who calls you, and He will bring it to pass." (1 Thessalonians 5:19, 20, 21, 24)

Finding God in Everything

"For the grace of God has appeared, bringing salvation to all men, instructing us to deny ungodliness and worldly desires and to live sensibly, righteously and godly in the present age, looking for the blessed hope of our great God and Savior, Christ Jesus, who gave Himself for us to redeem us from every lawless deed and to purify for Himself a people for His own possession, zealous for good deeds." (Titus 2:11-14)

When Jesus came into His hour of ministry on the earth, the hope of more than one man, even some of the disciples, was for revolution. It never happened in the ways they might have hoped, but it did happen. The years had passed, Jesus was now gone from the earth and the original 12 disciples gone as well, and yet the Gospel of Jesus Christ had continuously crept with fluid precision across the pagan world. Carried by the faithful feet of men like Paul, it was confirmed and established in the hearts and the daily lives of new converts through the ministering hands of men like Titus. He settled himself to live smack dab in the middle of this pagan community that had known nothing but idols. Although history and the daily lives of its people was void of anything that would seem to support the Gospel of Christ and the godly life that would soon accompany salvation, it grew among them. Men and women who knew nothing beyond the simple Truth that Jesus had died to give them life beyond their sin would eventually change all life as they, or their city, had known it. What does one do when everything old has passed away, and all things become new? Well, I think you set yourself to learn who He is, what He did and what that means to your life – both now and into eternity. The provision of God calls some to disciple and others to grow beneath their faithful care.

I'm dating myself when I tell you I learned to make stained glass windows and lamps in the '70's. Captivated by the process and the beauty, I bought a book and set myself to learn. Through the years I've not only learned a lot about glass, I learned some valuable lessons that have become spiritual principles to me in the years since. While doing my first small project, I decided to take a shortcut, leaving out one seemingly insignificant step I didn't understand the need for anyway. It was a tedious distraction and didn't make much sense. Its importance was not immediately apparent, and I was well into the project by the time I finally understood its purpose and realized it was too late to reverse it. My project was a failure. I kept that small piece for many years, letting it serve as a reminder that there is never a shortcut to excellence.

No one escapes the lessons that failure holds for it is the brooding companion of excellence. It shouldn't scare us so much to fail. Practice, which often leads to failure, is where boundaries are established, weaknesses exposed, methods perfected and excellence honed. Scripture does not feed us on the hearty victories of perfect men and women who remained unacquainted with loss or failure: Moses was a murderer, David an adulterer, Jacob a deceiver and Peter betrayed Christ. They knew seasons of failure, every one of them, but their faithful pursuit of excellence in both temporal and spiritual lives continually affirmed that God doesn't measure success by the number of failures that are numbered to our account.

Because of what Christ had done, those new converts under the care of Titus could find meaning in every circumstance and fresh purpose for every day. Grace did not measure what they had done, but what He had done. Did they too often get caught up in the old habits and accepted attitudes that had once accompanied their life and still flourished with neighbors, family, governments, and friends? Did they sometimes look for a shortcut to holiness because the importance of some Truth didn't make sense to them? I'm sure they did. Seeking the excellence of holiness is only a beacon that guides our path. To follow Him is a choice we make - and we will make it often.

It's easy enough to get so caught up in the process of life and our tendency to judge its merit and meaning that we forget to look for God in the midst of it. We might be surprised to find Him not only in those life-changing moments but the mundane, even the failures and losses our lives will know. Looking for Him, expecting to see Him, understanding that all things work together for good to them who love God and are called according to His purpose (see Romans 8:28) becomes the essential foundation on which we build a life-changing relationship with Him. Those who learn to live with an attitude that expects to find God in anything will find God in everything.

I finally threw my little *failure* away a few years ago. Not because I no longer needed to be reminded, it was simply time to let it go.

What He Freely Gave

"Jesus summoned His twelve disciples, and gave them authority over unclean spirits, to cast them out, and to heal every kind of disease and every kind of sickness. Heal the sick, raise the dead, cleanse the lepers, cast out demons. Freely you received, freely give. Behold, I send you out as sheep in the midst of wolves; so be shrewd as serpents, and innocent as doves." (Matthew 10: 1, 8, 16)

Jesus did not talk in circles nor was He illusive with the charge He set upon His disciples. "...He gave them authority over unclean spirits, to cast them out, and to heal every kind of disease and every kind of sickness."

I find the thought of living in this kind of authority a challenge that is equally encouraging and disconcerting for I live in a world troubled by evil on every side; one where disease robs health, finances, peace, and life from believers and unbelievers alike. The needs of humanity are apparent, to the point of overwhelming, and I seldom live in a level of faith that gives feet to the reality of faith that has authority over unclean spirits and heals every kind of disease...

The Words of Jesus often leave me wobbling between knowing every word He said is absolute in its Truth and possible for everyone who believes and then balancing it against the knowledge that believing it must inevitably require operating in it. The two are often separated by a gap that is not only wide but unsettling. Perhaps a good first step in comprehending this kind of faith must be to acknowledge that authority is not a choice we make to *have*; it's a choice we make to *seek* the One who gives it. Herein lays the fine line between faith and knowledge - the Source.

The search for knowledge will suggest to us there is an answer out there for everything: books, DVD's, seminars and teaching on positive mental attitudes and self-image. The premise of self-enlightenment seems to assume humans are self-sufficient, like little gods, equipped with an answer for every need, emotional stability, secure on each ever-ascending rung on the ladder of success and knowledge unending. The reality of people's lives contradicts the message which most often leads to *converts* who have become experts at denial and avoiding the truth with which their heart must surely convict them in the quiet moments. Perhaps that is because the reality of Positive Mental Attitude is that it is, at best, a weak imitation of faith; a trick played on humans, hoping to keep them from ever finding the Truth. Knowledge is still searching for the apple. "Now the serpent was more crafty than any beast of the field which the Lord God had made. And he *(serpent)* said ... For God knows that in the day you eat from it your eyes will be opened, and you will be like God, knowing good and evil" (see Genesis 3:1, 5).

There is nothing about faith in Jesus Christ that remotely identifies with a positive mental attitude.

The authority that rests in faith is not some convenience for our pleasure. It is not something one can learn to have, then ration out according to whatever presents itself and presses for resolution. It has no formula or principle that activates its power, is not "one-size-fits-all," cannot be worked up and although it is always consistent, it is rarely predictable. Though always on time, it is seldom timely - according to our human clocks - and seems to have quite a lot to do with the principle of *waiting*. It is unmovable from God's Word, must be borne by Grace that does not complain or run ahead, is a certainty that is rarely explainable, seldom understood. Faith is God working in the life of each, His Presence intensely personal and fit for every occasion, every need.

How does this translate to an authority that casts out and heals according to all that Jesus said? I think *authority* is merely assuming the right to use what He freely gave us. We have no responsibility to make something happen but to acknowledge His provision. That is not a particularly comfortable position for us humans who are drawn to pride, self-sufficiency, and need. The authority of faith asks us to lie down that He may be lifted up and allowed to flow through us - a willing channel for a purpose beyond our own needs. Our best example is Christ, who set aside His life, shed His Blood in obedience to the Father's plan; thereby opening the door to salvation and eternity to everyone who would believe on His Name.

The authority that comes with faith is not a *handle* by which we move God to our bidding according to need or circumstance – faith lives beyond circumstances. Authority looks at the realities of life and denies them the power to have their way; it accompanies that moment when our heart, mind, and soul aligns with God's Word and speaks what He has said.

Rehearsing Life Before Him

"Rejoice always; pray without ceasing, in everything give thanks; for this is God's will for you in Christ Jesus. Do not quench the Spirit; do not despise prophetic utterances. But examine everything carefully; hold fast to that which is good." (1 Thessalonians 5:16 - 21)

Looking through one of my old notebooks, I found this writing, "Lord, I feel so alone – I feel so discouraged, I have waited so long for an answer…" (I, I, I, blah, blah, blah.) It made me laugh at myself. Now, I cannot remember the exact circumstance that brought that out of my pencil back then but today's response of my heart makes it a solid reminder that prayer often becomes too much about the "I need…" and not nearly enough about the "You are…."

Perhaps I considered something similar that day as well, for immediately following was written, "My Lord and Heavenly Father. Thanks for being so close to me today. I know I can tell You anything. You know me; know the depths of my heart and the cares that often linger there. You do not condemn my flesh for being weak or my heart for caring. You are…"

Perhaps many of us struggle at times with prayer. We wonder if we're doing it right, if God hears us, hoping somehow the words we say hold power, will affect the change or answer we seek. It is said God answers every prayer, the more immediate response is "yes", "no" or "wait" and most of us are left feeling that the answer most often forthcoming is "wait." Perhaps that is because God sees farther down the road than we. That should be sufficient motivation for releasing the heart-wrenching care and concern we feel from seeing, hearing and carrying more than we want to see, hear or carry. Our mind may know that faith is the ingredient called for at this crucial juncture – but our heart often forgets in Whom to put our trust.

Let us consider a few things we probably know but of which we often need to be reminded:

(1) Prayer is not just a *meeting* we have with God; one at which we hurriedly arrive and quickly get it over with so we can get on with our day. Those moments spent with God are important; could be, should be, moments we intentionally set aside to worship Him, rehearsing both the joys of life as well as the cares we set before Him. Prayer is primarily an attitude of being connected to the Father through and by the redemptive Blood of the Son, borne upon the wings of the Holy Spirit.

(2) We are one with Him – connected; not for the moments that begin, "Dear Heavenly Father" and conclude with "Amen" but always, each moment of every day. We are the temple of the Holy Spirit; He abides within us! Our life becomes part of prayer, every moment an occasion to present to Him our cares and joys. This heart we call our own beats in time with the cadence of His Life that dwells within.

(3) As with Paul, we learn - are learning - to be content in whatever circumstances we are (see Philippians 4:11). Living content should be a vital concept to us: one that reflects our ultimate trust in the Father. Trust has acknowledged that He sees, knows and answers every prayer and every concern out of His vast storehouse of

wisdom, vision, and purpose, and in a perfect and timely manner. Once acknowledged, we should then be able to relax and set our self to living our moments from that position – trust.

Being able to release one's life into the hands of another, even the Lord, will challenge most of us day by day, sometimes moment by moment. It's not natural to our flesh to trust in that which cannot tickle our senses or assure our emotions. Some moments we will see Him clearly and get it right. Some days we remember that prayer is not so much about rehearsing before Him the needs and answers we desire but sharing life and conversation; not for set-aside moments, but in the hours that stretch beyond the set-aside moments.

(4) Do not approach God like He is *out there*. He is *out there* but because He indwells this tent of flesh by the power of the Holy Spirit, this house redeemed by the shed Blood of Jesus Christ, the One that is *out there* is also *in here*. Let us live aware that we take Him into every situation, every problem. If our feet, heart, or mouth has gone there, He has gone with us. It's almost beyond our willingness to comprehend that when we are angry, hateful, shady or thoughtless; we have taken Him with us. If we speak His Name in the company of sinners, we have taken Him with us. "Let your character be free from the love of money, being content with what you have, for He Himself has said, 'I will never desert, nor will I ever forsake you.'" (Hebrews 13:5) We share this dwelling place, this body that is for today called home. For this, I am especially grateful for some of my most profound prayers have no words – only my spirit that groans my heart's desire to the One who knows me completely and loves me well.

Strengthen Your Stakes

"Enlarge the place of your tent; stretch out the curtains of your dwellings, spare not; lengthen your cords, lengthen your cords, and strengthen your pegs." (Isaiah 54:2)

I think my favorite book, certainly in the Old Testament, is Isaiah. Isaiah penned his words to and about people who quite consistently let their life choices run toward rebellion; his message confirming hope in God, no matter the trouble man might have made of the day. Isaiah knew that no matter what the people did, or how they lived, the purpose of God had not changed, nor had His Promise diminished.

Israel was made up of people who knew a lot about God; it did not always translate that they knew God. How they saw God, the degree to which they believed Him, made the defining difference in the quality of their lives, their attitudes and actions affecting life-choices, and the integrity with which they conducted themselves; all of which influenced their future. God's plan for man has always been the same: (1) Love the Lord, your God (2) Abstain from evil (3) Live under His cover and from His provision. Israel's history is rich and diverse. With neighbors like Egyptians, Babylonians, and Assyrians, war and tumult were, at all times, either a genuine threat or an absolute reality. When the people walked in the ways of the Lord God, He was their cover and their help. When they became lovers of their own way, enamored with their own choices, He lifted His hand of protection and care, letting *life* become their teacher.

By 715-687 B.C. under King Hezekiah, Isaiah - meaning "may the Lord save" - was called by the Lord as a prophet to Israel. He was an unusual choice, in that he came from a family of means and was familiar with the Temple court in Jerusalem. These experiences gave him a broader view of history and the politics of the day; his discernment regarding them was that both were merely tools serving God's plan for the final redemption of man. He served as Israel's prophet through the reign of three kings. One of them Israel's' worst, Ahaz, an evil ruler who submitted to the Assyrians to the point of degradation when he replicated their pagan altar in the Temple at Jerusalem; and the son of Ahaz, Hezekiah, one of Israel's best and most godly kings.

That Isaiah lived in perilous and troubling times, there is no argument. The government was untrustworthy and failed the needs of the country and its people, the rich were lovers of self and money, and the poor were pawns and servants of both the rich and the government. War and threats of war worried the hearts of the people, wickedness abounded – but for a remnant of godly men, always God raises up a portion within whom the Promise is carried forth into the next generation. Isaiah so believed in the promise that dwelt with the remnant that He named his son, Shear-jashub - meaning "a remnant shall return". It was here in the midst of what was the most troubling of times that Isaiah spoke the Promise of Redemption.

I would suggest that now might be a superb place to stop reading for a moment and read the whole of Isaiah, chapter 53. You will find within these verses a compelling and prophetic picture of the Son of Man, Jesus Christ, who "...He Himself bore the sin of many, and interceded for the transgressors." (Isaiah 53:12b) It was upon that foundation that Isaiah laid the prophetic stones of the promised Messiah. He looked forward to the reality of His coming, the liberty and fulfillment it represented, as surely as we look back.

Little has changed from his day to ours when we consider the affairs of man. I think a newspaper from Isaiah's day would read much the same as the one delivered to your door or the one that came via your "app." But to the remnant, to those who still believe in the Promise, the news does not affirm the measure of any season! Isaiah prophesied that we should always live with an attitude toward strength, provision, and increase and a future He - not current events - has prophesied. "Enlarge the place of your tent; stretch out the curtains of your dwellings, spare not; lengthen your cords and strengthen your pegs. For you will spread abroad to the right and to the left. And your descendants will possess nations, and they will resettle the desolate cities." (Isaiah 54:2, 3)

Historically, we live in a day of restoration as Israel is once more fulfilling the Word He spoke regarding their beginnings and their end. Spiritually, He has grafted in those who name the Name of Jesus Christ as Lord and Savior; including them in the Promise and all it holds. As children of God and heirs of salvation, we are part of the remnant because of the shed Blood of the Messiah of which Isaiah prophesied and whom we know and serve.

Because of Practice

"Although He was a Son, He learned obedience from the things which He suffered. And having been made perfect, He became to all those who obey Him the source of eternal salvation, being designated by God as a high priest according to the order of Melchizedek." (Hebrews 5:8-10)

A mother Chipping Sparrow brought her baby to my feeder today. Getting ready to push him out of the nest, she was teaching him to fend for himself; but, although the baby was as big as she, he made no move toward securing a portion for himself. I watched with interest at his constant demand upon her, standing with beak agape, moving in rhythm with her so she could not avoid notice. There was food in abundance right before him but not once did he help himself; allowing, even demanding, that she feed him.

In the 5th chapter of Hebrews, Paul had a similar dilemma. Much of what He writes there is laying down the spiritual foundation for Jesus as our High Priest. Everything about Jesus was purposeful, intentional and a fulfillment of established prophecy and authority. When Paul said He was of the order of Melchizedek, he was referring back to Genesis 14, to the king of Jerusalem and priest of the God most High. Before his name was Abraham, it was the high priest Melchizedek who blessed Abram, he to whom Abram paid his tithe. Paul was establishing the priestly lineage of Jesus to a people of whom he says, "Concerning Him, we have much to say, and it is hard to explain, since you have become dull of hearing." (Hebrews 5:11)

I think most of us can be, at times, just as capable of being dull of hearing as those who Paul refers to in Hebrews. When we get too busy, too caught up in the cares of life, or distracted, our hearing seems to be the first to go. We tend to stop listening for the sound of His voice, to stop hearing anything but the rattle of our thoughts and emotions. It's a common enough problem and one any of us can be found guilty of it on occasion. But a momentary distraction from the maturity that is the cornerstone of spiritual authority is very different than what Paul calls a sign of immaturity. When he says, "Though by this time you ought to be teachers, you have need again for someone to teach you...you have come to need milk and not solid food." (Hebrews 5:12) He's saying they were acting like spiritual babies, putting their spiritual lives at risk because, "But solid food *(spiritual Truth)* is for the mature, who because of practice have their senses trained to discern good and evil." (Hebrews 12:14) This Truth is vital if we are to maintain our spiritual equilibrium and safety. We have an enemy that delights when you choose to pretend evil does not exist; he dances with glee over those who barely skim the surface of the plan of Redemption, assuming themselves to be safe. It is an evil plan that would pervert the Truth and water it down with a goal to separate you from every gift, authority, and heritage; all that has been set in store for you and your generations according to God's plan and promise. Would anyone cast their inheritance away because it somehow seemed more comfortable to remain aloof, ignorant or apathetic?

Because their lives had been redeemed by the Blood of the Lamb, because of His spiritual heritage and position of authority, they - as do we - had the same rights, privileges, and authority as He. But, having rights, privileges and authority does not translate to change in the life of one who continues to stand with my young Sparrow, mouth agape and waiting to be fed.

I remember a time when I prayed to the Lord to "know more." Inside of me these words of rebuke washed over me as I heard Him say, "You don't need to know more; you need to do what you already know." I think that's what Paul meant when he said, "...who because of practice have their senses trained..." (see Hebrews 5:14). Maturity in Christ is never attained by what we have come to know; rather, by consistently *putting into practice* of the Truths He has revealed to our spirit and enlightened to our heart. Sometimes the journey from head to heart is long and treacherous; but, one who has "...because of practice have their senses trained to discern good and evil" would not be easily undone. Having learned how to *listen*, it becomes more critical that we know how to *hear*. Even when we get caught in the trap of boiling emotions, we know not to live there. When we know He is the authcrity, and we are His hands, His lips, and His feet; we know to begin practicing His presence. Be continually refreshed by the knowledge of our High Priest; for He has abundantly planted His gifts within us – and they are sufficient for every occasion.

We Don't Live there Anymore

"Pay close attention to yourself and to your teaching; persevere in these things; for as you do this you will insure salvation both for yourself and for those who hear you." (1 Timothy 4:16)

Suddenly aware of a pair of black eyes looking at me and a similarly black nose pointed my way brought my attention back from the thoughts that had so certainly kept my reflections elsewhere. Our dog, Murphy Brown, wanted her morning walk. Not a hard request to accommodate, we headed out the door. There's a definite nip in the air, so I made a quick detour inside for a jacket. Signs of life, slowly fading, catch my eye; patches of red and gold dot the landscape, the perfect backdrop for the one lonely leaf that dances its way to the ground on the crisp morning breeze. I love the changing of the seasons, finding them a comforting testimony that the cycle God set in motion follows His command with faithful diligence.

In many areas of our life the same can be said: the choices we make, those that once they've been firmly planted in Him, bear fruit; the seed multiplied, allowing us to plant in still greater abundance. This Truth does not always translate with the same ease as the cycles that order the seasons. If able to stand upon the mountain-top of rejoicing over the harvest a season has brought, it is very likely the planting of it took place in a valley. Although I love the mountain-top of victory and have learned to appreciate the trials, losses and hard spiritual work of the valley experiences, my greater hope is that I more consistently dwell in the balance that hangs between the two.

Like most of us, I was born into the family of God with a long string of baggage wanting to come along for the ride. Some freeloaders were more evident than others and quickly enough set by the side of the tracks; some not so much. For me it was the emotional baggage, the patterns, and habits of conditioned response that would often raise their inner voice, causing me to react in fear, shame or uncertainty. From there it was a quick transition from new-found peace and growth to a spiraling cycle of despair. Everyone has trying days that sometimes lead to unwanted memories; if, however, you are given to repeating a pattern of the same rise followed by the same fall - that constitutes a cycle.

Cycles are those reoccurring patterns that regularly revisit, usually when we least expect them or are prepared to overcome them. They typically run deep and are often destructive, having become a long-established habit of response, most often springing from our emotions. Hardly noticing the trigger that sets it off, we may find ourselves under a spell that could last for hours, days or weeks before we recognize our self as under its control. It ceases to matter whether the spiral is up, causing a sense of hilarity that precedes unwise choices, or down, causing depression, defeat, anger, and self-absorption, cycles will continue to vex our soul, undo our resolve. Eventually, they entice us to a double-minded life where we make excuses, allowances or become adept at hiding. Self-will doesn't have the tenacity or wisdom to face down a cycle for long; its tendrils go too deep into the past for us to completely understand its beginnings. That its purpose is the destruction of our will and eventually our soul is rarely apparent to one caught in its devices. It becomes adept at demanding we accommodate its presence, so we say, "This is just the way I am." Well, it might be the way *we were* - but it is also a part the Blood of Christ paid to redeem, and we don't have to live there anymore.

When life lies beyond our ability to make the best decisions for ourselves, He is there! The attitude and honesty with which we face our need is the first step in overcoming bondage; becoming aware is the first milestone of defeating the web of sabotage the enemy of our soul has laid. Only the Lord has seen the whole of our journey; those hurts, unwise choices, unbidden words and experiences that stung our soul and damaged our hope. Only He can plot a safe course over the obstacles of doubt and fear that will throw themselves in our path. His will for us is that every part of us – *every part* – be redeemed. He paid for it all! Our willingness to submit to the journey is the only variable; for following the awareness, comes the work: reading His Word, the discipline to deny those familiar paths of response, forgiving our self, building new emotional habits that allow for better choices. It takes time and diligence! We need not face this journey alone for He has promised to be there, to cover, encourage, help, lead and persevere with us through every trial or cycle with which we find ourselves hindered – all the way to deliverance and redemption of our life, our peace, our portion.

The Beggars Bowl

"And knowing their thoughts, He said to them, 'Any kingdom divided against itself is laid waste; and any city or house divided against itself will not stand." (Matthew 12:25)

Anyone who is a follower of Jesus Christ has most likely heard the argument, or accusation, that Christians are weak and looking for something to prop up their needy existence. I suppose in a particular regard there is a small seed within their observation that does ring true. One of the most significant strengths of the people of God is their honest acceptance of how frail we humans are and how in need of something beyond ourselves to rely on for revelation, understanding, insight, peace, strength, perseverance and finally, eternity. It is more honest to call it wisdom, for they have merely acknowledged a genuine need.

No matter the degree or measure of delusion with which we may try to reinforce our self-sufficiency, every man/woman looks to something for significance, respite or help. Some give themselves to work, the building of a storehouse of resources that offer the illusion of safety. Some continue to search; driven by shifty invitations that promise a bit of peace from incessant demand their soul makes upon them for something – anything – to feel significant and to stop the voice of accusation. It's unsettling to face the realization that the path of life upon which we had set our feet had led to nowhere.

Where does one go from there? Well, we either continue on the road to nowhere – or we take the leap.

Each of us who have called upon the Name Jesus Christ - to save us from our sins and our past choices in exchange for a future and hope – has leaped. It takes a considerable degree of courage, the kind that is rarely acknowledged, to examine our life and admit that eternity requires more of us than we have to give. Courage faces the fact that this earthly kingdom in which we had once planted our hope is not only divided; it has been laid to waste. It's true; we are weak and looking for something to prop up our needy existence.

It's not unusual that Christians will work as hard, laugh, cry and love as much; have as many problems with health, family, and relationships as those who live without His Grace; but because the motivation of the heart is different, the results are different as well. A life that has so honestly faced the realities of what it holds is one that bears witness to the only choice that matters: have we planted our life and our eternity in a "what" or a *Who*?

Most people do believe in God (or god), perhaps hoping to create Him according to their own need or concept, giving Him attributes and qualities, trying to bring Him down to a level they can understand. They construct rules they can follow, feeling comfortable in the deluded sense that they have a certain amount of control over their appointed days and what comes after it. The Person of God does not change because Man attempts to deny Him, control Him, put Him in a box, or script Him like He was the marionette and we were pulling the strings. It does, however, change the one who would seek to constrain Him.

We often forget we live in a world where sin has long been practiced and has grown to a very efficient model of destruction; one which spawns perversion, immorality, disease, dysfunction, and pain set abroad in the earth. Man demands the right to cast his seed into the field of his choosing and screams "Unfair!" at the day of harvest.

Jesus spoke about a house divided to the Pharisees, the most religious and devout men of His day. They knew only rules and lived consumed by them, sacrificing compassion on the altar of rote, paupers of emotion at the plight of the ugly and the lost, they cast their pennies into the beggar's bowl and dusted his cries from the finely woven cloth of their shoulders. Setting themselves apart, they hid behind the letter of the Law; thereby becoming a house divided against the reality of a life poured out to God.

Between these various extremes stands the Lord and Savior, Jesus Christ, the One who will shed His Blood for both. It does not matter that the one comes in rags, the other in finely woven cloth. "For we are all as an unclean thing, and all our righteousness are as filthy rags, and we do all fade as a leaf; and our iniquities, like the wind, have taken us away." (Isaiah 64:6) We all need to be saved – from the world, from sin, from ourselves. No matter what our hope or our need, He completes us. When our world is dark, He is light. When we are hungry, He is Bread. When we are sad or alone, He is our Comforter. When we are divided, He restores. In every need, His Grace is sufficient.

The Other Side of Love

"For this cause a man shall leave his father and mother, and shall cleave to his wife, and the two shall become one flesh." (Ephesians 5:31)

Because we live much of life within the context of relationships, - family, friends, marriage - maintaining individuality within them becomes critical. Losing sight of who we are diminishes the quality of any relationship. We need what others bring to our life; others need what only we can contribute to theirs. I'm always intrigued by the circle of people that surround each of us, considering myself blessed by those who add those certain unique ingredients that flavor my life, build and challenge me, make me laugh, think and grow. I have been enriched and eternally changed because of the influence they have had on my life. We tend to seek these people out, want to be with them because they enrich us. By adding to our measure, expanding our awareness, interest, and experience, they permit us to grow, be comfortable in who we are and what we have to give; holding us accountable to our fullest potential in the process. That we would live in relationship has been God's design since Man's beginning in the Garden when He said, "...It is not good for the man to be alone..." (see Genesis 2:18). We need people, do immeasurably better when we feel loved, approved, encouraged and safe. The strength of a healthy relationship is born out of the principles of trust, respect, flexibility, and compromise.

I guess *love* sometimes has another side to its coin. Sometimes love is stingy, bound by conditions that denies approval when one will not bow to the will of the other. Sometimes it tries to control; that usually administered through anger which is either heated or icy cold. It's a torment for both, I think; a form of destruction that seems to wait for the moment that final line is crossed. It's a near impossibility for the one being controlled to remain full of energy and life because of the constant pressure to relinquish their individuality, actions, and personality into the control and dictates of another. I think some would try to conform to what is required of them and it might seem to work - for a season. The more important it is to us to maintain approval, the harder and longer we will try, but slowly our true self will begin to dim and slowly slip away. I think it the height of arrogance that any would presume to treat one God's creation as chattel, possessions to be owned and therefore remodeled according to one's pleasure or need; especially when administered under the guise that it is out of love. The lack of honor that exists when one must serve the other's gaping need to own or control holds within it the seed of eventual destruction for any relationship.

We need people; need others to bear us up during times of loss, distress or life-choices every person must make. No one has sufficient resources to render them always capable of sound decisions for their own lives, let alone another they seek to control. We all need counsel or a listening ear sometimes. Our most natural source of advice is our mate, friends or family. But, any confidence must rest on a foundation of trust, respect, compromise, and flexibility. If there is any doubt that those things will not be returned to us in kind, we'd best keep our lip zipped.

Life is tough, demanding and often uncertain and we do it best within a community. The strength of any relationship does not come from tight-fisted control that demands one must serve the other; preferably, from letting go to the higher truths of love and respect, treating the other as we would desire to be treated. There is more wisdom, strength, experience, and capability in two and "...a cord of three strands is not quickly torn apart" (see Ecclesiastes 4:12).

I hold to the principle that submission is a Biblical principle. I also believe the motive of the one who might *require* it will have a great deal to do with whether it works as intended – or not. I think Paul covered it well in Ephesians when he admonished wives to be subject to their husbands - as to the Lord, - and men to love their wives as their own bodies, to nourish and cherish them as Christ does the church (see Ephesians 5:22-30). A high calling for both, I think, having nothing to do with who's in control.

That a wife would elect to live in submission to her husband in no way infers that she is lower than he or less capable; but rather that she has willingly chosen to serve the same kind of love and care that Christ gives for His church. It is a wise man who will encourage his wife to bring her very best to his household and life, to add her wisdom and experience to his own. This kind of love does not constrain but covers, confirming that he is stronger and more complete because of the gifts she brings. Submission should allow both to leave the authority in a relationship where it belongs, in Christ. A man is then left free to cover his wife and her to be his helpmate.

First Love

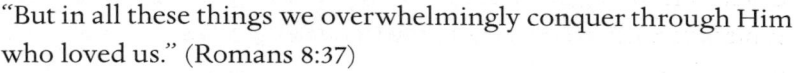

"But in all these things we overwhelmingly conquer through Him who loved us." (Romans 8:37)

Somewhere in the quiet of this morning, I found myself – amazingly so - in the middle of one of those days that doesn't happen often; a day when no one needs something of me, and I am left alone with my thoughts and prayers. In the middle of being surprised by this rare occasion, I found myself drawn to remember earlier and busier days, experiences, things I had learned and ways I had served the Lord. It's been many years now since I've come to know Him as Lord and Savior, have walked in His ways, serving Him and the church. My reflections left me wondering how much of what I've done has increased the harvest and how much had merely churned the chaff.

I think it easy enough for us to lose our focus on what is truly important, genuinely requires our time, our energy, our heart, and how much is just busyness that checks off the "Service" box and quiets the guilt we are often so good at practicing. Guilt doesn't need much practice for it seems to flow quite naturally from the accuser's tongue and we've heard it long enough that it seems we automatically consider it. We do a whole lot better at keeping our time and gifts channeled to those areas where they will be most effective when we keep our First Love in mind, you know, the One whom we love and serve. It's easy enough to become so buried in the busyness of service that we defer our love and genuine praise to the fleeting moments that exist between one activity and the next. When we take a moment to consider, we know that our heart still burns with gratitude for our load of sin He took upon Himself at the Cross; that He dwells within our temple of flesh and has written our name in the Lamb's Book of Life. But, the gratitude is fleeting, so often weighed down somewhere in the busyness of our journey that most of the joy of it has leaked away. The day to day often wears us thin. If you can say the same, then perhaps both of us need to get intimately re-acquainted with our First Love.

To maintain a healthy and loving relationship with the Lord will require us to keep awareness, confession, and repentance as close and life-long companions. David declared, "I waited patiently for the Lord; and He inclined to me and heard my cry. He brought me up out of the pit of destruction, out of miry clay; and He set my feet upon a rock making my footsteps firm. And He put a new song in my mouth, a song of praise to our God; many will see and fear, and will trust in the Lord." (Psalm 40:1-3)

Paul said we should "Do all things without grumbling or disputing; that you may prove yourselves to be blameless and innocent, children of God above reproach in the midst of a crooked and perverse generation, among whom you appear as lights in the world." (Philippians 2:14, 15)

Believers cry out to find the equilibrium that rests with God in a world that muddies the lines. We often find ourselves divided into two camps: too much interest in the troubles of life and not enough. Either way, trouble is a reality in our "crooked and perverse generation." Trouble **has** visited - **is** visiting - or **will** visit our life, making some seasons particularly tough, answers to prayer seemingly slow in coming. So, what's new? Do we think God's plan suddenly changed? Giving an audience to the voices that proclaim that evil is strong, and God has somehow become weak never changes evil - it only changes us because we cease to respond to life with faith. It is not a lack of faith that admits we live in a fallen world that boasts trouble on every side. Faith sees things as they are but acknowledges He is sufficient and through Him, we are still more than conquerors.

Living in a world that is not our eternal home (see John 17:16) requires us to choose this day whom we will serve (see Joshua 24:22).

And so it seems that the days now before us, with all of its bad news, will remain a constant buzzing in our ears and our flesh will sometimes lean toward its clamor. To whom will we listen? To whom - or what - we will give our answer; and thereby our power?

These are the moments and the place to which God has called us, the place He becomes real to us. Right here in the midst of this noisy, confusing, demanding, beautiful and sometimes horrific sea of humanity is God. He seeks, saves and sustains those who answer His call. Neither our best or worst days move God from His purpose - that we might know Him by the shed Blood and saving Grace of His Son, Jesus Christ.

Who Said You Were Naked

"...Do not fear or be dismayed because of this great multitude, for the battle is not yours but God's." (2 Chronicles 20:15b)

Having just eaten of the fruit of the tree of the knowledge of Good and Evil, innocence submitted itself to a lesser plan and shame became their portion, for the eyes of Adam and Eve were opened and they knew themselves to be naked (*exposed*). "And they heard the sound of the Lord God walking in the garden in the cool of the day, and the man and his wife hid themselves from the presence of the Lord God..." (see Genesis 3:7, 8). I find it interesting that sins' first response was to hide from God. "And He said, who told you that you were naked? Have you eaten from the tree of which I commanded you not to eat?" (Genesis 3:11) Then the man blamed the woman, and the woman blamed the serpent, and the serpent just smiled. And there is the very first pattern for what we humans often do after getting caught in our sin.

A world created for fellowship, provision, and peace became indebted to shame, fear, and blame. And, God wrote the plan that would enable Mankind to reclaim what had been his intended portion from the beginning. Choices, once made, always change the ingredients of the plan. Because man's choice became disobedience, he lost the covering, knew himself to be naked, and God's intended plan forever changed. The penalty: man would live his days under the curse, given to sorrow, toil, trouble, and death; the woman to know the pain of childbirth and live under her husband's authority.

"The Lord God made garments of skin for Adam and his wife, and clothed them." (Genesis 3:21) God did not abandon them to their hasty choice, He covered them, but He also sent them out of the Garden. Life outside was a battle to which they had been neither called nor prepared; but then, that is often the price of free will that does not count the cost before it chooses. Perhaps the plight of Adam and Eve is not so unusual, other than that they were the first of a long line of humans that answer the serpents' subtle questions with words that roll from a prideful tongue. They were ill prepared to meet the consequences.

"Therefore, just as through one man sin entered into the world, and death through sin, and so death spread to all men because all sinned." (Romans 5:12) It would be many generations before the man, Christ Jesus, would redeem this evil seed of death and separation that was planted into the lives of Mankind because the serpent "…was more crafty…" (see Genesis 3:1).

Having been born under the curse, all humans are subject to loss and sin, in need of redemption. I wonder if women ever give a silent sigh of relief that the Lord gave them an opportunity to right what had been a prideful blunder through the first hint of the Savior; One who would be born of woman, who would bruise the serpent's head (see Genesis 3:15). God never left us without a plan. Whether looking forward to or back to the Cross, He has always made a way of redemption and restoration for all who would seek Him, believe Him and walk in His ways.

The Old Testament is all about the battles we face when seeking to reclaim what God had intended as our portion in the first place. The people spent most of their days fighting for peace, but they learned to seek God for direction. If they chose not to look to Him, they soon discovered the other side of consequence. God had promised them a *land*, but while making it their own, Israel would know great victory and great defeat. Their attitude and diligence toward seeking God made the difference regarding what part of the battle was theirs – or if they had a part at all. God doesn't change; it is always His desire that we seek Him for every occasion and every battle we face. Wisdom would look to resources beyond our own, I think.

2 Chronicles 20 lays out an excellent example of how to approach a battle God's way: (1) King Jehoshaphat acknowledged and defined the enemy. (2) He acknowledged his fear and set himself to seek the Lord. (3) He gathered believers to pray. (4) He rehearsed God's help. (5) The Spirit of the Lord came and spoke to him, "...Do not fear or be dismayed because of this great multitude, for the battle is not yours but God's." (2 Chronicles 2:15)

I think the greater enemy here was not the Moabites but the fear they faced; fear they acknowledged and rolled onto God. To do so challenges pride and flesh, for they will scream for us to charge first and pray later. We often do charge wildly ahead, somehow hoping God will cover whatever we do as long as we do something. Fear is an old and wily foe, and its threat requires more of us than just showing up to the battle. And, "When they began singing and praising, the Lord set ambushes..." (2 Chronicles 20:22)

Every contest will ask us where we have planted our fear: in circumstances or in Him who rules over them.

In Pursuit of God

"Seek the Lord while He may be found; call upon Him while He is near. Let the wicked forsake his way and the unrighteous man his thoughts; and let him return to the Lord, and He will have compassion on him...for He will abundantly pardon. 'For My thoughts are not your thoughts, nor are your ways my ways,' declares the Lord." (Isaiah 55: 6-8)

With so many seeking to find the wisdom of God, to know Him, to hear Him speak, hoping to validate life, beliefs, and direction how many of us find that for which we are looking? Is God hard to find? Are we looking in the right place, asking the right questions? Are we afraid the answers might cost more than we are willing to pay? What does He want? What does He expect from us? Although it is true that He has already given the answers we seek, made the provision to fulfill our heart's desire, only those who diligently seek Him will find Him. What does it mean then to *diligently* seek Him? Only a journey set to finding out will answer both our questions and our calling.

When my husband and I were young and dating, still playing games and finding our boundaries, he once said this to me, "Don't ask the question if you don't want to hear the truth." I've never forgotten that and it has served our relationship very well. Early on I learned he was not all about playing games. He was genuine and expected the same from me.

I've found the same principle holds true in my pursuit of God, His wisdom, His purpose and my life-calling in Him. God loves me, He loves you too, both without measure; but He is not about playing games. He is not merely *after* the Truth; He *is* the Truth. Don't ask the question if you don't want to hear the Truth of His answer.

Sometimes it is too easy to play at knowing God. We want salvation, to go to heaven when we die. We want Him to answer our prayers and meet our needs, carry our burdens and make our children turn out well. We don't always take our part as seriously as we assume His to be. It is way too easy to pass right over those "seek ye first..." and "...deny yourself" parts. It's easy enough to skim the "forgive" parts. The truth is that knowing God will cost us everything we think to be our own, everything we think we know and everything we neatly listed as our prayer goals and our expectations. If one were to pick up my Bible, it would give an accurate picture of those first days that formed my patterns of belief. You are way more likely to find His promises underlined in the "God will" parts than the "you will" parts. Most days I've grown beyond that - most days. When we take into account the whole of Scripture, the parts that say we will know times of trouble and have fiery trials, we're not so overcome when they show up. Learning this truth allows our faith to become planted further down the road to the place where the Promise is fulfilled. We're not so prone to keep our eyes on the middle, where the details are being worked out.

To pursue God will require us to ask the tough questions of ourselves, but do so with an honest heart, one willing to make the sacrifice the answer might require. To ask the hard questions regarding our soul demands an ear set to hear the Truth.

The time we give to our journey will either be our enemy or our friend; it depends on what we make of it. I suggest we must consider any time we give grudgingly to people, prayer, service, meditation or reading His Word *has been lost already*. Add to that the time spent in regret and reliving the past. Whether those times were satisfying or terrible, they are gone and we cannot wish them back. Only memories remain, and whether we celebrate a victory or bemoan a loss, nothing gives them life once more. They can only serve as a counselor to the present – a present whose moments we are called to redeem.

How easy it seems to forget we are but vessels - vessels filled, restored and renewed – only as they are poured out. That with which God supplies us was never meant to be ours. We have the water of His Spirit - people thirst. We have His Grace - they are naked and cold. We are redeemed – the lost clamor to be found. We have gifts – the buckets of the world are empty. We have Bread - hunger abounds. A vessel never owns what it contains; perhaps the only thing it might call its own is the choice to pour. The reality that presents itself to our comfortable lives is this: will we, or will we not?

We are never alone in those times we are called to serve Him. He is always our counsel and our Guide. If we listen, we will hear, for there are needs we are called to serve - and some we are not. Learn to discern the difference. We are not called to meet every demand, just those He brings before our storehouse of supply. "Then Jesus said to His disciples, 'If anyone wishes to come after Me, he must deny himself, and take up his cross and follow Me. For whoever wishes to save his life shall lose it; but whoever loses his life for My sake will find it." (Matthew 16:24, 25)

Trusting the Voice

"In Him, you also, after listening to the message of truth, the gospel of your salvation - having also believed, you were sealed in Him with the Holy Spirit of promise, who is given as a pledge of our inheritance, with a view to the redemption of God's own possession, to the praise of His glory." (Ephesians 1:13, 14)

I think it a weighty consideration to know God included us in such words as *sealed, promise, pledge, inheritance and surety*. Although He has promised; it still falls to us to choose whether we will walk in that provision. When God speaks to us, are we able to move beyond our fears, our need for comfort and the assumed safety of what we think we know? Can we trust we truly hear Him and understand what He requires of us? What if we fail Him because of the fear? What if we get it wrong? Can we believe He means what He says? Time and experience will affirm that, yes, we can entirely trust Him – although rarely in the ways we might have imagined. And, as long as we stay the course, we won't get it wrong. The Holy Spirit dwells within us to help perform His Word. We can trust that He will help us get it right. Anyone wishing to know about God's provision and intent toward each one of us will find it written in the Book of Ephesians.

His ways will always seem beyond our complete understanding so a lot of what we know must be accepted by faith, regarding the revelation and wisdom he freely gives. We might as well agree that our flesh, that *natural man* will argue the foolishness of faith, accusing that we are not only wrong but puny and fearful as well. Our flesh tells us to trust the fear. We will soon have to make a choice about which voice to believe.

May it be the God of our Lord Jesus Christ, who gives us:

- A pledge of our inheritance, with a view to the redemption of God's own possession
- A spirit of wisdom and of revelation in the knowledge of Him
- Eyes of our heart that they may be enlightened
- To know what is the hope of His calling, the riches of the glory of His inheritance in the saints
- The surpassing greatness of His power toward us who believe (see Ephesians 1:13-19).

There's nothing wretched or puny about one who walks in the wisdom of such a promise.

Our inheritance includes a wealth of wisdom, revelation, understanding, enlightenment, and power that remains untested, underdeveloped and mostly unused. One might as well conclude that He has made a lot more provision available to us than we could ever use.

God the Father, put "...all things..." under the feet of the Son, making them subject to His authority (see Ephesians 1:22). Because we are the Temple of the Holy Spirit, because our house of flesh has become His earthly dwelling place, it follows then that He is both the covering and authority for those things we see and feel - and the unseen powers of darkness we do not see - but are real, none-the-less. Although they stand defeated, they do not go quietly. He stripped them of power, so the only power they have left is what we give them to work with: the fear, doubt, and sin we leave unchecked in our lives. The most significant contribution we make to our own torment is the choices we make to remain ignorant of what the Bible says about our position of authority in Christ. We cannot avoid the battle between good and evil, and we cannot effectively meet the battle when we choose to remain unarmed.

"Therefore take up the full armor of God, so that you will be able to resist in the evil day, and having done everything, to stand firm." (Ephesians 6:13) Those are words of war. He has equipped us in every way possible, promised He would not leave us nor forsake us, to prosper us in those things we need and cover us with His authority; but those provisions only come as we walk covered by what He has provided. Our part in a life of authority: (1) To believe His Word is Truth (2) Acknowledge that the world and the devil do not wish us well (3) Put on the armor He's provided (4) Stand firm!

Those are the unfailing riches that will keep us, no matter what the economy does, through the darkest of days, the fiery darts of the wicked, principalities and powers and every scheme of the devil or man. We have an inheritance in Him. It is out of that provision we, and all within our care, are kept.

A Poorly Knitted Garment

"But you are a chosen race, a royal priesthood, a holy nation, a people for God's own possession, so that you may proclaim the excellencies of Him who has called you out of darkness into His marvelous light." (1 Peter 2:9)

No matter the circumstances of our beginning days, regardless of whether our initial input was nurturing or not, it is likely we will never come to appreciate our unique individuality until we can agree with Genesis that each of us came into being by design. Intentional, perfect in purpose and plan; a *chosen* possession called out of darkness into marvelous light – His marvelous light. "God created man in His own image, in the image of God He created him; male and female He created them. God blessed them; and God said to them, 'Be fruitful and multiply...and rule...over every living thing.'" (Genesis 1:27, 28) Created in the image of God, our spirit is that essential part of our individual and unique being that is *of* God and *from* God by intentional and specific design. It is He that blew upon that finite cell and gave it life that is now eternal. That seed within came fully equipped for all that life will require of us – each characteristic, gift, ability and the wisdom to perform it. Denial, sin, disgrace, unworthiness or unbelief changes nothing but our own hope in a future.

How curious that once born, as unique and individual as our initial design might have been, we spend so much of our time seeking to fit in, or be one of the crowd; for the crowd tends to reject anyone who dares to be different. The initial demand *the crowd* requires is compliance to their normal, and the threat of being ostracized is very real to those who resist. I think the crowd mentality must spring from a deep sense of fear and insecurity, for some small measure of comfort accompanies the same-ness of the masses. Almost any form of acceptance somehow verifies to the seeker that he/she belongs, so must be all right. One will never be pressed by undue challenge toward excellence, individualism or creativity by *the crowd*, for uniformity gives the illusion of safety and acceptance. It's not a position that one, stirred by a soul created in the image of God, can long endure.

Given enough life-experiences and God's glorious Creation soon resembles a poorly knitted garment; a stitch dropped here and there, loose ends, runs and gaps in the fabric of who we are and what we might have been. It is no surprise that we need to be redeemed from what life and our interpretations of it have knit into our soul. Thankfully, God remembers our original design, the intent and purpose He planted within the spirit of every child into whom He blew Life. When we call upon His Name, He settles within and begins the process – as we can and will allow – of reknitting our soul. It may take some time and a lot of unraveling of those hastily cast stitches, but whom better for the process than He who knew us and drew us before we were conceived in our mother's womb.

It gives no glory to our life or to the God who claims us as His own to deny our gifts or contributions and sink into the illusion of what only looks like safety. What might be safe about any place that requires such a sacrifice? God fit each of us with a specific skill set. Some have minds that envision great and mighty things, which another will build and yet others will operate. The world is a needy place and you are an answer, right in the place where you dwell with what is at your command to be and to do. Let us not hold back our hand from being the difference.

There are lots of ways we attempt to satisfy that innate part every man/woman recognizes as a void waiting to be filled. Some search for God, for a spiritual sense of becoming complete; some only a god that will quiet the clamor and fill those empty parts, those devoid of satisfaction and will not be denied. "And coming to Him as to a living stone which has been rejected by men, but is choice and precious in the sight of God, you also, as living stones, are being built up as a spiritual house for a holy priesthood..." (1 Peter 2:4, 5) These words reflect that part of the nature of every human that first calls us then compels us to seek Him - to know and be known by Him - to be built by Him, to be like Him, to reflect Him. Accepting that we are *of* God allows our soul to rest in the knowledge that we are but sheep awaiting the shearing; that we might be carded and spun, as fine wool into – a garment reknit.

What Did You Go Out to See?

"He who has ears to hear, let him hear." (Matthew 11:15)

Perhaps every generation from the Creation of Man, has considered themselves to be a bit, more likely a lot, more contemporary and progressive, having grown beyond the authorities that formed their beginnings. It's a mystery that humanity, thinking they have come so far, have stayed so singularly the same in the process: ever seeking but rarely stopping to savor, they wait for something that will change the day-to-day, the mundane or hopelessness of their existence, often missing it when it presents itself before them.

Historically, the people looked for and awaited the Messiah, but when the days of Mary were accomplished, it passed unnoticed by all but a few. Both the Message and the messenger arrived as babies, stayed by the Father's hand until the day eternity groaned and He set His eye toward accomplishing His eternal purpose. I'm sure John cut quite a figure with his camel-hair shirt and leather girdle, baptizing in the river. Though second cousins, John and Jesus had met but once, and that as babes within their mother's womb when they leaped, and John was filled with the Holy Spirit. Years later, Jesus stood aside and watched as John was questioned about who he was. John replied, "I am the one crying in the wilderness, 'Make straight the way of the Lord' as the prophet Isaiah said.'" (John 1:23) The next day he saw Jesus coming to him as he was baptizing in the waters of the Jordan River at Bethany, and said, "...Behold the Lamb of God who takes away the sin of the world!" (John 1: 29) When Jesus stood before him, John put his hand upon Him and immersed Him in the waters. "Now when all the people were baptized, Jesus was also baptized, and while He was praying, heaven was opened, and the Holy Spirit descended upon Him in bodily form like a dove, and a voice came out of heaven, 'You are My beloved Son, in You I am well-pleased.'" (Luke 3:21, 22) From that moment the days of Christ's ministry on earth had begun; three years that would transform history and, in turn, eternity.

We now live in a world of social media, days when few escape unwanted pictures and words that make casual inferences or record every move. In that light it is thought-provoking to consider that John and Jesus passed for an ordained moment in time then went their separate ways of ministry and did not see each other again. So controversial was John in his preaching, Herod Antipas eventually sent soldiers to arrest him. Wishing him dead but fearing the face of the people who now lived awaiting Messiah because of his message, John waited for the news he knew would come. From prison, he sent his disciples to ask Jesus, "Are you the Expected One...? Jesus answered and said to them, 'Go and report to John what you hear and see: the blind receive sight and the lame walk; the lepers are cleansed and the deaf hear, the dead are raised up, and the poor have the Gospel preached to them. And blessed is he who does not take offense (*stumble over*) at Me.'" (Matthew 11:3-6)

He was indeed the Expected One, but many did stumble over Him. When their expectations included an *expected who* - earthly king, leader - who would accomplish an *expected what* - earthly deliverance from the bondage of their life - their expectations of Him became their stumbling block. Perhaps that's some of what Solomon pondered when he wrote, "Watch over your heart with all diligence, for from it flow the springs of life." (Provers 4:23) Any time our needs or expectations – heart - rise to a place of priority, the shift of the flow has begun.

Expectations blind us to the purpose that lies beyond what we see in the moment. Humanity hungered for something or someone who will fill the need as they saw it. Giving credibility to their expectations:

- Colored the reality of what they saw
- Soon gave way to judgment regarding the deeds of John and Jesus - the Truth
- Rendered them blind to the redemption that stood before them.

Then three times Jesus questioned the crowd regarding John and the message he brought, asking them what they had gone out to see. (See Matthew 11:7-9) To what purpose does any man chase after such a messenger: for the Truth, hope and personal change of it, or the momentary diversion from the ordinary, and the expectations of the crowd? Jesus went on to compare that generation to a group of children in the market place, playing their games, pouting, spouting their discontent. To which He answered, "...yet wisdom is vindicated by her deeds." (Matthew 11:19) Perhaps it does not matter so much how we initially see or hope Jesus will be, **but what we do with Him** when He comes before us. Always that choice awaits our making and ultimately Eternity requires that we choose. So many had seen the miracles, enjoyed the show and hung on the fringe with an unrepentant heart. Refusing to choose, they had made the choice already.

The questions He asks are never to *them*. It is *we* who hear a word softly spoken, "But what did you go out to see?" The answer awaits the question. "He who has ears to hear, let him hear." (Matthew 11:15)